Your Astrological Life Compass

A Modern Guide to Astrology, Psychology & Well-Being

Your Astrological Life Compass

A Modern Guide to Astrology, Psychology & Well-Being

Frida Ilahi

London, UK
Washington, DC, USA

First published by Mantra Books, 2026
Mantra Books is an imprint of Collective Ink Ltd.,
Unit 11, Shepperton House, 89 Shepperton Road, London, N1 3DF
office@collectiveinkbooks.com
www.collectiveinkbooks.com
www.mantra-books.net

For distributor details and how to order please visit the 'Ordering' section on our website.

ISBN: 978 1 80341 801 8
978 1 80341 898 8 (ebook)
Library of Congress Control Number: 2024912327

A CIP catalogue record for this book is available from the British Library.

Design: Lapiz Digital Services

UK: Printed and bound by CPI Group (UK) Ltd, Croydon, CR0 4YY
Printed in North America by CPI GPS partners

Contents

To all the creative visionaries who once felt like idiots while paving new paths

Introduction

I was first introduced to astrology a few years before becoming a psychologist. Before that, my only reference to astrology was horoscopes in magazines based on generalized Sun sign interpretations. Many people believe that astrology is limited to what you read about in these magazines, and that astrology is primarily practiced by women, which I used to believe too. My understanding of astrology changed when I was introduced to this ancient art through an old boyfriend of mine. He and his father were practicing astrologers and used astrology to interpret and understand life. I can still remember the first time they showed me a horoscope. I was intrigued. It looked so different from what I had thought. So complex but still so simple at the same time. My then-partner explained that a horoscope is like a snapshot of the sky during a particular moment and that there is a symbolic meaning connected to the positions of the planets and the 12 zodiac signs. He spoke the astrological language, used words like "conjunction" and "exalted," and referred to the planetary energies as symbolic of different things in daily life. One of the things that immediately interested me about astrology is that it is like a language, which is based on the interpretation of energies via ancient glyphs. There is an esoteric element to astrology, as proper interpretation requires knowledge to decode the glyphs and interpret the energies through knowledge related to symbols and archetypes. The fact that this knowledge is so ancient and still sort of "hidden" immediately caught my attention.

Until quite recently, I considered my interests in astrology and psychology as distinct and separate subjects. After graduating from the psychologist program in Sweden, I started working in the field of adult psychiatry — and not even once did it cross my mind ever to use astrology as a tool in the clinical setting. Why? Because it just isn't allowed. Although I understand the need for regulations and I support most rules, it has always baffled me how some people almost seemed obligated to criticize me based on their belief that my interest in astrology could somehow impact my professionalism, harm people, or threaten my ethical responsibilities as a psychologist. For years, I walked around with guilt and shame for liking astrology. Reflecting upon this, I can now observe my experiences through another lens. I now understand that most people do not know "real" astrology. I understand that many people in my field are very biased and tend to believe that practices need to be scientifically validated to have value, even if they are used outside of the clinical setting for private reasons. The idea that my professionalism as a psychologist could be threatened due to my passion for astrology is somewhat absurd, though — at least if you ask me.

Nevertheless, I know many people who, like me, have walked the academic or scientific path and struggled to "come out" and be proud of their esoteric, unscientific interests. That mirrors our rigid society and strict societal norms more than anything else.

Thinking that I would start reading people's horoscopes in the middle of a therapy session would be like assuming that a lawyer passionate about dancing would start dancing in the courtroom. It simply does not make sense. However, this is how many people think, and I believe that this is what has created a stigma around psychologists or therapists who are interested in astrology. On the other hand, some might rightfully wonder how it is possible to separate these two practices since they do, in fact, share several mutual characteristics. The answer to this is that I believe in openness, discussion, and awareness. I also firmly believe that the stigma around astrological practice may have pushed some astrology-loving psychologists and therapists to operate "under the radar," despite not being allowed to do so. I personally know of psychologists and psychiatrists who believe in the value of astrological practice but who are unable to step forward and speak up due to fear of the repercussions that might come with that, at least in Sweden, where I am located. "They could recall your license. Are you not scared?!"

This book is the result of having had one foot in science and one foot "beyond" for more than a decade. It is my sincere attempt to show that it is, in fact, possible to integrate astrological practice with psychology and to do so without shame or guilt. I believe in the potential of merging modern astrology with psychology and exploring this integration from a well-being perspective. Ultimately, I also want to pay my respects to astrology as a subject since it has sprinkled its magic upon me for so many years by showing that it is, in fact, not just about generalized interpretations or attempts to predict the future. Astrology is so much more than that! The same applies to psychology, which is not just about diagnosing psychopathology or curing mental illness. Through broadening the perspectives, I hope to provide you with a fresh look at how to work with these two practices through an ethical, practical, and "trans-scientific" approach. I want to demonstrate how the horoscope can function as a life compass, much like the ones therapists use to help their clients live a more fulfilling life. By shifting our focus from seeing the astrological energies as a measure of "strengths and weaknesses" and instead exploring our *values*, we can build an integrative approach where the horoscope and the energies in our chart help us reflect upon *our values* and find a *valued direction in life* — beyond shame, guilt, and rigidity. In this book, I will introduce you to my way of pairing astrology with modern, evidence-based psychological concepts to promote well-being — without falling into dogmatic interpretations or getting stuck in scientific rigidity. You will be able to work practically with your chart and begin to use it as a life compass to promote well-being. I will show how the planets relate to modern psychology and how identifying the planets by sign and house placements can help you find a valued life direction that could help you gain a greater sense of overall well-being.

Chapter 1

Astrology, Psychology, and Ethics

Let us begin by defining what we mean when we mention astrology and psychology. Astrology and psychology are two distinct fields that study human behavior and functioning. While astrology can be defined as a *belief system* built on the idea that celestial bodies influence human affairs, psychology is the *scientific* discipline that explores the mind, behavior, and emotions through empirical research and structured observations. Astrologers can provide alternative guidance based on a *horoscope,* while psychologists offer professional support to improve *mental health.* Today, psychology has established itself as a *science,* while astrology falls under the categorization of a *pseudo-science.* Psychologists need to provide proof of adequate education and training and must base their practice on methodologies with scientific support, while also adhering to a strict ethical code of conduct. By contrast, astrological services belong to an unregulated market with close to no obligations at all. Despite this, I often think about astrology and psychology as two twin sisters. Both fields do, in fact, exhibit similar characteristics and tend to mirror one another in a variety of ways. Practitioners within both astrology and psychology tend to seek to understand and describe human behavior – while also incorporating elements of guidance, advice, and counseling.

As a psychologist, I have often been confronted with how I can be interested in astrology. It is almost as if some people cannot grasp how I can choose to stand with one foot in the scientific world while also practicing astrology – a pseudo-science?! I think this stems from the notion that, as psychologists, we must adhere to a strict code of ethics that governs our professional behavior and the treatment of our clients. This code often includes guidelines on ethics, confidentiality, boundaries in therapeutic relationships, and the duty to report any potential harm to clients or others. We demonstrate our commitment to providing quality care to those we serve by meeting these requirements and upholding these ethical standards. In addition to this, we are also taught that the boundaries between personal beliefs and professional conduct must be maintained to ensure the highest level of care and ethical standards. But where do we draw the line here? Should I not be able to be interested in astrology just because it is not labeled *scientific*? Should I feel ashamed for liking astrology just because I happen to have a doctoral degree in psychology? To me, that sounds like *scientism*, that is, the belief that only science is valuable.

I am aware that my experiences could sound like an exaggeration to some — I mean, why would it not be okay for me to practice astrology? Aren't we allowed to have a life outside our profession, too? After having been through this process for over a decade, I can honestly say that the stigma surrounding psychologists or scientists who practice astrology is a complex issue that I believe stems from the perceived clash between scientific rigor and esoteric beliefs. I know I am not the only one who has experienced this stigma; there are many of us who share similar experiences. I think this stigma is rooted in the belief that any involvement in astrology could impact a psychologist's professional practice or ethical responsibilities. The stigma might lead psychologists and similar professionals to hesitate to openly share their interests in the esoteric, which could be linked to various reasons, such as the fear of being misunderstood or judged by colleagues. I have spent many years feeling ashamed and worried about what others would think if I revealed my passion for astrology. I have also been told I should "be careful" so that no one knows about my love for astrology since that could potentially "ruin my whole career." Statements like these have helped me shed light on the fear of professional repercussions, as esoteric interests are often considered "outside the mainstream" and not aligned with traditional scientific or evidence-based practices.

On the other hand, I have also unexpectedly met people who were supportive and curious about my passion for astrology. I remember one time at my old job in adult psychiatry when one of the psychiatrists approached me after I acknowledged my interest in astrology. She handed me a small Post-it note with her birth details and kindly asked me if I could take a look at her chart. This was a turning point in my life as it helped me realize that most humans, despite their academic papers and titles, share a common curiosity through an interest in the more esoteric side of life. That there are many more, just like me, out there.

Where the Two Practices Meet

The focus on how to live a good life is one area where the practices of astrology and psychology intersect, mainly because many people interested in astrology also tend to be interested in psychology and how to live a more meaningful life. The question about how to live a more meaningful life has historically been covered by ethics, moral philosophy, or structured religion through principles such as the Ten Commandments or other religious or philosophical texts aiming to provide people with a structure for how to live their lives in the most fulfilling way. In a contemporary, Western, more secularized context, we might turn to the science of psychology to explore how to live a more meaningful life.

Although most of today's mental health interventions are based on and supported by science, methods such as Cognitive Behavioral Therapy (CBT) have also been criticized for sometimes being too mechanical. In general, CBT methods tend to be criticized for failing to address the concerns of the "whole human," which, in combination with the fact that millennials and Gen Z might be more secularized than previous generations, could make astrology eligible as a holistic method that could satisfy a "void" that organized religion and modern psychology might currently fail to address. Today, astrology is often talked about as a wellness tool with self-help characteristics, and it is not uncommon for people to know their "big three" (i.e. their Sun sign, Moon sign, and the sign of their Ascendant). When I started studying astrology almost 14 years ago, I did not know anyone interested in astrology outside of my small circle of dedicated astrology nerds. Now, I can meet people in the street, and when they hear that I am an astrologer, they immediately tell me their most prominent astrological placements. Astrology is facing a renaissance, and the question of how to live a more meaningful life is highly relevant.

Astrology Is Not Fortune-Telling

Despite astrology's current renaissance, most people still think of astrology as fortune-telling or simplified astrological columns in weekly magazines. Among astrologers, we would refer to this type of astrology as *Sun sign astrology*, and it is not uncommon to hear critics refer to this definition when trying to debunk astrology's relevance. But if astrology is not fortune-telling, what is it?

In short, astrology is an esoteric language based on understanding the symbolism of planetary energies and how they manifest themselves through us here on Earth. In addition, astrology is often described through the phrase "As above, so below," which illustrates one of astrology's fundamental principles: external events (i.e. the positions of the planets) are thought to impact us in our human experiences. There are many different branches of astrology, and what most people perhaps do not know is that Sun sign astrology is a relatively new branch of astrology and was first invented sometime in the 1930s, while astrology as a subject dates back thousands of years. In ancient times, astrologers were often highly educated, skilled astronomers and mathematicians who could guide others – often those of high social status. In ancient times, people turned to astrologers because they knew how to calculate a horoscope and deliver an interpretation accurately. Historically, astrology faced a downfall during the scientific revolution as it was formally rejected and categorized as a pseudo-science. The church further opposed the recognition of astrology through the advancements of structured religion. This is interesting, considering that astrology is now facing a rebirth, as anyone can draw up their horoscope with the help of websites or mobile applications, which has led to the global astrology market growing immensely. Some analysts link this development to the Coronavirus pandemic, when more and more people turned to astrology as a way to cope with "luxury boredom" while also navigating uncertainty or despair. This recent development was perhaps most prominently seen in the Western world, with millennials and Gen Z turning to astrology apps and astrologers on social media to understand and explore life. While I and many others highly welcome this development, I also believe it raises essential questions about astrological practice and how to practice astrology ethically in a modern context. The idea that we could see a psychologist to learn about ourselves is slowly being complemented by the notion that an astrologer can provide the same kind of guidance. The fact that these two disciplines are very different in their relation to scientific relevance calls for essential questions to be asked. One such question could be how we can use astrology as a self-help tool while also integrating the scientific advancements of modern psychology. Another question could be how to marry these two disciplines ethically in a contemporary context. How can we explore astrology and psychology so that it becomes fulfilling, exciting, and fun? And how can we enjoy astrological practice without legitimizing it in scientific terms, and without denying what the science of psychology has taught us about human functioning?

Since I am an astrologer with an educational background in psychology, I can use my psychological knowledge of human behavior to offer more nuanced interpretations of astrological charts. From my perspective, I see much therapeutic potential in the "magic" related to astrology, and this is perhaps why I advocate for integration. When I say "magic," I refer to the fact that many of my astrological clients feel very seen and understood based on the information retrieved from the astrological chart. "How come you knew that about me?" or "You confirmed what I have been feeling for years – how?!" are examples of this phenomenon. These are also the kinds of holistic experiences that might provide a counterweight to the critique that contemporary CBT methods have received for sometimes being too mechanical and failing to address "the whole human."

What Is an Evidence-Based Psychological Practice?

As you might have noticed, I use the term *evidence-based* to describe modern psychology's position in relation to science. But what do we actually mean when we say something is "evidence-based" in relation to therapeutic methods? According to the American Psychological Association,[1] the term *evidence-based practice in psychology* (EBPP) refers to an integration of three main components:

1. the best available research
2. clinical expertise

[1] American Psychological Association. (2021). Professional Practice Guidelines for Evidence-Based Psychological Practice in Health Care.

3. consideration for the client's characteristics, culture, and preferences.

In plain English, *the best available research* emphasizes the importance of relying on scientific studies to make informed decisions about the most effective strategies for addressing mental health issues and promoting well-being. This means that the methods we use as psychologists have been tested and proven to work. By grounding psychological practices in evidence-based methods, we strive to ensure that our therapeutic interventions are supported by research through rigorous scientific testing. As mentioned, this perspective contrasts with astrology since astrological interpretations are *subjective* rather than *scientifically validated*. I want to be clear, however, that this does not mean that astrology could not be proven valuable by science. That is possible, but it would require stepping away from a positivistic view of science by going beyond the simplicity of whether astrology "works" or "does not work."

Second, *clinical expertise* refers to the competency of the clinical experts responsible for the interventions. The third component, *consideration for the client's characteristics, culture, and preferences*, highlights how psychological services are most effective when they correspond to the client's specific problems, strengths, personality, sociocultural context, and preferences. This also includes sociocultural and familial factors such as gender, gender identity, ethnicity, race, social class, religion, disability status, family structure, and sexual orientation. It also includes environmental factors such as institutional racism and healthcare disparities, and — perhaps most importantly — personal preferences.

Simply put, this means that a client's personal preferences, such as values, beliefs, and worldviews, are known to be related to therapeutic outcomes. This perspective aligns with recent developments in the diagnostic manuals that psychologists and psychiatrists use to assess and diagnose psychopathology. You might not know this, but as psychologists, we are entitled to use specific manuals to diagnose psychiatric disorders. Over the past decades, considerations regarding religion and spirituality have been added to these manuals, meaning that spiritual or religious worldviews have been acknowledged as nonpathological. In plain English, this means that if you believe in fairies as part of your spiritual worldview (and this belief does not prevent you from functioning in daily life), then this is not, per se, a psychiatric problem; that is, you are not crazy because of believing in something that goes beyond the tangible realm of existence. This might sound obvious to many of us today. Still, we need to remember that the mental health field has a heritage of more than a hundred years of ignoring or even pathologizing the influence of spiritual or religious experiences, including astrology. Connecting this to the modern astrology of today, it can be argued that astrology is indeed a form of spirituality since it could be considered a belief system. Those of us who follow astrology as a spiritual practice know that it has the potential to provide a sense of meaning, comfort, and insight while also providing guidance and adding purpose to our lives. From this perspective, hostile comments such as "But how can you be interested in astrology when you're a psychologist – you should stick to science instead!" could be seen as an issue related to freedom of beliefs rather than an attack on personal values and interests. Knowing what I know today, I wish I had answered accordingly to those who questioned me in the past, possibly by stating, "Freedom of belief is a fundamental human right and a crucial role in ensuring a diverse and inclusive society." Considering that the client's characteristics, culture, and preferences could help bring better results to the therapeutic setting makes it less controversial to potentially pair scientifically proven therapeutic methods with modern astrology, don't you think?

What Psychology Can Learn from Astrology

While it might be favorable to use therapeutic methods and interventions that have been evaluated in scientific studies, there is also a critique against EBPP (evidence-based practice in psychology). Such a critique has also been proposed by modern thinkers, who highlight how modern psychotherapy is influenced by "scientism," that is, the belief that only science can provide legitimate knowledge. The idea that modern psychotherapy is, in many ways, a normative practice that imposes the idea that some ways of living are preferable to others is central to this idea. This critique highlights evidence-based practice in psychology (EBPP) by demonstrating how it does, in fact, *not* consist of three equal components (i.e. best available research, clinical expertise, and the client's characteristics, culture, and preferences) but instead consists of one overarching component (best available research) with two subordinate categories (clinical knowledge and the client's characteristics, culture and preferences). Ultimately, this perspective claims that modern psychiatric practice seems to fail to "walk the talk," and further stresses that there is alarmingly little criticism of evidence-based psychology today.[2]

My own experience concerning this issue comes from having worked as a clinical psychologist in adult psychiatry in Sweden. The clinic I worked at had profiled itself as a "scientifically orientated clinic." Although I strongly believe in the power of science, I also witnessed how the practical implications of this approach failed to be helpful in a more practical, everyday context. An example of this was when the clinic's management team decided to restructure the therapy methods offered by its practitioners. It was stated that

[2] University of Bergen. (2020.09.15). The problem with evidence-based practice in psychology. https://www.uib.no/en/svt/138353/problem-evidence-based-practice-psychology

everything needed to be done with the most robust possible evidence, meaning that the practitioners would have to adhere to stricter rules about what methods they were allowed to use when working with patients. Therapy in group format was dismissed and removed from the offered methodologies since it was stated that unified methods targeted to groups had less evidence than individual therapy methods aimed at specific problems. This was surprising, as I had seen how the group format had helped many people heal. I personally considered the group therapies successful based on my observations and the data derived from evaluations. However, that format needed to be sufficiently supported by science, and, therefore, it was removed.

On a similar note, despite all the conversations about scientific rigor and evidence-based practices, I had never heard of the importance of evidence-based practices combined with clinical expertise and the client's characteristics, culture, *and preferences.* I would say that my experience was that the clients had little to no influence on their treatment or what methods we provided. That was not anything that we would discuss or take into consideration. I am aware that patients suffering from mental health issues might not always have the strength to influence the choice of methods in a clinical setting. However, I do believe it is essential to meet each person where they are, which is also implied by the American Psychological Association's policy document about Evidence-Based Psychological Practices (EBPP). Whether modern psychiatry manages to do so today is perhaps a whole other discussion. In conclusion, I think it should be more widely accepted to work with multimodal approaches for clients who wish to explore life from a "trans-scientific perspective," as long as they do not require urgent psychiatric care. Perhaps through a therapeutic approach involving astrology or other esoteric practices?

What Astrology Can Learn from Psychology

People come to astrologers for guidance, and we should be aware of what impact an astrologer can have during a consultation. While I do not deny that individuals without formal education or training can create a positive impact when guiding others, it could be important for an astrologer to at least be trained in the basics of human functioning. Similarly, I believe professional astrologers should follow some code of ethics to prevent causing unnecessary harm to the clients they meet. Most professional astrologers emphasize the need for ethics within the astrological practice. However, despite that, I have also encountered several astrological practitioners who have said and done things that could be considered highly *unethical*. When discussing what astrology can learn from psychology, I immediately think of awareness around power imbalances. Talking about power imbalances between the client and the therapist is a common practice within psychology. When considering these power dynamics, it is crucial to recognize the inherent imbalance in the relationship between the therapist and the client. Psychologists are trained to acknowledge that they hold a position of authority and expertise, as clients may find themselves in vulnerable states, seeking external help and guidance. This power dynamic could influence the therapeutic alliance and impact the client's ability to engage and express themselves fully.

The same goes for the astrological setting, particularly since the astrologer can interpret the astrological language – a skill the client might lack. I remember the first time I had my chart read. It was terrifying! I looked at the horoscope before me and observed all the glyphs and houses. I remember wondering what the astrologer could see about me that I could not see *myself*. "What will they say about me?" With that anticipation comes the potential for the astrologer to impact the client's life positively or negatively. This is an example of a power imbalance in the astrological setting, where the client might wonder what the astrologer can see about the client that they are unaware of themselves. Most professional astrologers will do their best to adjust and bring balance to these dynamics. However, I have also been to a few astrologers who seem to thrive because they know something that the individual across from them does not know. I believe there is a need to discuss ethical questions surrounding the practitioner-client relationship also in astrology. The ethical frameworks developed in psychological and psychotherapeutic practice can thus be important for astrologers to take inspiration from.

Merging Astrology with Psychology for Well-Being: Why and How?

Although the pairing of astrology and psychology is not new, merging astrology with modern, scientifically supported psychological concepts of well-being is an area that has yet to be explored. Before we start exploring *how* this could be done, defining what we mean when we refer to *well-being* is essential. According to the World Health Organization, well-being can be understood as a positive state experienced by individuals and societies. It includes quality of life and being able to contribute to the world with a sense of meaning or purpose.[3] In terms of mental health, the WHO highlights how *cognitive health* is more than just the absence of mental disorders; it is an integral part of health. Having said this, we understand that health is a broad construct with many layers.

I believe that the stigma around psychologists or therapists who practice astrology is simply because we still have not found a way to integrate these subjects to combine scientific findings with the esoteric. To explain what I mean, I would like

---

[3] World Health Organization. (2024). *Promoting Well-Being*. World Health Organization. https://www.who.int/activities/promoting-well-being

to draw a parallel with another research field that is becoming more popular in the Western world — the study of Psychedelic-Assisted Psychotherapy (PAP). Some scientists expect that psychedelic substances will become evidence-based treatment options in regular healthcare within the upcoming ten years. That is quite a development, particularly since I can recall sitting next to psychiatrists and nurses at my former job who were lecturing me about how extremely dangerous these substances are and how immensely stupid it is to believe that they could bring any *therapeutic value*. Times are indeed changing, and that is fascinating.

Nevertheless, as with all changes, we must adjust our expectations and practices to align with the current knowledge. Another excellent example of the current development of integrating perspectives comes from the field of parapsychology (PSI), which is the study of *paranormal* or *psychic phenomena*. This research has a history of being somewhat controversial as it includes studying various abilities such as *telepathy, clairvoyance, precognition,* and *psychokinesis* — abilities that historically have been met with skepticism from the scientific community. At the same time, recent years have brought a growing interest in applying rigorous scientific methods to study these kinds of phenomena, as more and more researchers have been conducting experiments using controlled conditions, statistical analyses, and replication studies to investigate the existence and nature of "PSI abilities." These advancements have led to a better understanding of the potential mechanisms underlying parapsychological phenomena and have sparked debates about the nature of consciousness and reality. Overall, PSI and PAP continue to evolve, with researchers striving to bridge the gap between the paranormal, the alternative, and the scientific. While there is still much to uncover and explore, these advancements offer a unique perspective on practices that used to be considered "fringe movements." What if the potential integration of psychology and astrology could follow a similar development?

Astrology and Traditional Psychology: Why or Why Not?

Psychology and astrology also mirror each other through the many sub-branches within these subjects. Psychology, like astrology, is a broad subject with many underlying areas of interest. One of the best known is perhaps what we refer to as *traditional psychology,* which has a history of being primarily focused on identifying the causes and symptoms of mental illnesses and emotional disturbance. This framework includes diagnosing *psychopathology,* curing *mental illness,* and *decreasing dysfunction* through interventions aiming to bring individuals from a deficit point (i.e. -8) to a baseline for human functioning (i.e. 0). Simply put, this means to "treat" or "cure" people who are feeling depressed or anxious so that they can get back to a functional state.

In my opinion, combining this kind of psychology with astrology may raise specific ethical concerns, as the traditional psychological framework is primarily focused on curing mental health issues. Even though some astrological practitioners might advocate for the use of astrology as a tool for identifying potential markers for mental illness or personality disorders, my standpoint is that astrology is not suited for these kinds of pursuits. It can also be discussed whether an esoteric (and potentially inclusive) practice like astrology should be used to identify those who tend to fall out of "normative functionality." Is that how we want to engage with astrology? In particular, norms and "normal/normative functionality" are concepts that we have created, which means that the majority of our psychiatric diagnoses' expressions of non-normative functionality are based on existing societal norms. Although some astrological practitioners might claim that it is indeed possible to find markers that mirror specific psychopathological symptoms, the question of whether that kind of practice is ethical or not remains.

We need to remember that psychiatric diagnoses can evoke stigma, but also that individuals with potential undiagnosed psychopathology might be extra vulnerable, which requires safe methods for assessment and treatment. Sadly, some people might turn to astrology to "self-diagnose." While I can agree that psychiatric diagnoses are different from somatic/medical diagnoses and are therefore less robust to begin with, I must again emphasize how psychiatric diagnoses are always related to an assessment of *functionality*. An effect of our increased societal demands could be that more people seek help and ask to be assessed for their perceived difficulties. Although getting a psychiatric diagnosis can be helpful for many, I believe it exceeds the scope of astrology since astrology, in my opinion, is better suited to help us see how we all *belong* — rather than how we *differ*.

Despite psychiatric diagnoses being criteria-based and therefore less robust, we also need to remember that licensed psychiatrists and psychologists have undergone extensive training to diagnose these conditions. Similarly, psychiatrists and psychologists use diagnostic interviews, psychometrically valid rating scales, and multimodal approaches when assessing potential psychopathology — which is not the case with astrology. Their assessment model also often includes a whole team of several professionals with a wide range of insight into a patient's life. Despite this, I have sometimes observed astrologers claiming to know what astrological markers are linked to specific psychiatric diagnoses. One of the most discussed diagnoses is perhaps Attention Deficit Hyperactivity Disorder (ADHD), which is characterized by inattention and hyperactivity. As an astrologer, I can understand the curiosity involved in linking these diagnoses to the astrological chart.

However, as a psychologist, I know how complex these diagnoses are and how much time goes into assessing these conditions. The fact that some astrologers seem to believe they can identify ADHD symptoms based on planetary positions or aspects in the astrological chart is concerning, not only because it diminishes the complexity of the assessment process but also because astrology is not scientifically proven to work as a diagnostic tool.

Astrology and Positive Psychology: What It Is and How It Differs from Traditional Psychology

A contrasting perspective to traditional psychology is *positive psychology*, which includes the scientific study of what makes life worth living and what makes people thrive.[4] According to some prominent researchers within the field, the absence of suffering will not inherently promote well-being and joy, but will instead help remove a barrier and make it more attainable to experience through concepts such as pleasure, engagement, and meaning.[5] In plain English, this means that if we only focus on decreasing suffering, we might struggle to live a whole, content, full life where we *thrive*. Although focusing on "decreasing our suffering" can work as a pathway to start living a more fulfilling life, positive psychology advocates that *actual* development is fostered by understanding that we also need to ask ourselves what *promotes* well-being instead of just seeing what makes us suffer.

---

[4] Peterson, C. (2008). What is positive psychology, and what is it not? *Psychology Today*. Retrieved 2024-03-03 from https://www.psychologytoday.com/us/blog/the-good-life/200805/what-is-positive-psychology-and-what-is-it-not

[5] Duckworth, A. L., Steen, T. A., & Seligman, M. E. P. (2005). Positive psychology in clinical practice. *Annual Review of Clinical Psychology, 1*, 629–51. https://doi.org/10.1146/annurev.clinpsy.1. 102803.144154

Contrary to the traditional view, this branch of psychology is more inclined towards identifying strengths so that an individual can go from a plus point to an increased level of well-being. We can refer to this as "thriving rather than just surviving." Within this psychological framework, the focus on curing what is ill is replaced by a focus on increasing what is *well and working*. This is done by identifying forward-looking thought patterns, behaviors, and experiences that can improve what is well and what makes life worth living.

Scientifically, psychologists and social scientists have argued from several perspectives to define what makes humans thrive. Some perspectives include the belief that in order to feel content and function optimally, we must experience not only an absence of negative emotions but also the presence of positive emotions, social connections, and trust.[6] Pioneers in well-being and positive psychology, including Martin Seligman, have presented other, complementary perspectives. Seligman's model PERMA, which stands for *Positive emotions, Engagement, Relationships, Meaning, and Accomplishment*, stems from a mix of a *eudemonic* framework (e.g. happiness is an overarching theme) and a *hedonic* framework (e.g. happiness is about feeling good) and identifies these five areas as essential indicators for well-being and a happy life.[7] I personally believe that positive psychology is an excellent match to pair with astrology as it does not focus on curing what is ill but instead aims to *boost, favor,* and *grow* what is well and working through identifying strengths, virtues, and values. I also believe that it would be less ethically sensitive to combine this type of psychology with

---

[6] Butler, J., & Kern, M. L. (2016). The PERMA-Profiler: A brief multidimensional measure of flourishing. *International Journal of Wellbeing, 6,* 1–48. https://doi.org/10.5502/ijw.v6i3.526

[7] Seligman, M. E. (2012). *Flourish: A visionary new understanding of happiness and well-being.* New York: Atria Paperback.

astrology as it would include identifying character strengths and values through astrology, as opposed to diagnosing psychopathology or treating mental distress.

Positive Psychology: Two Main Perspectives

As I briefly mentioned above, within the field of positive psychology there are two main ideas known as the *eudemonic* and the *hedonic* frameworks. These are two different but overlapping perspectives within modern well-being research. The hedonic framework focuses on the importance of pleasant and comfortable states and experiences, while the eudemonic perspective highlights living a good life and being fully functioning through purposeful living.[8] The eudemonic and hedonic perspectives date back to ancient Greek philosophy, as the idea of hedonic happiness originated in the fourth century BC with the Greek philosopher Aristippus, who promoted *maximizing happiness*. The eudemonic approach originates from the same period but was first proposed by Aristotle in his work *Nicomachean Ethics*, where he highlighted the importance of leading a life based on one's virtues in order to attain a purposeful life. *Eudemonia* refers to a life of fulfillment where happiness is more of an overarching effect linked to living a life according to one's purpose rather than *a goal*.

In this book, we will lean on both perspectives to understand what makes life worth living. I have long been interested in philosophy and studied moral philosophy briefly before entering the psychology program to become a psychologist. The idea that

---

[8] Ryan, R. M., & Deci, E. L. (2001). On happiness and human potentials: A review of research on hedonic and eudaimonic well-being. *Annual Review of Psychology, 52*, 141–66. doi: 10.1146/annurev.psych.52.1.141

Ryan, R. M., Huta, V., & Deci, E. L. (2008). Living well: A self-determination theory perspective on eudaimonia. *Journal of Happiness Studies, 9*, 139–70. doi: 10.1007/s10902-006-9023-4

happiness is not a "goal in itself" but rather an effect of living a life in accordance with virtues or values was intriguing when I first heard about it. I remember the professor explaining how the ancient Greek philosopher Aristotle claimed that all things are ends in themselves (intrinsic) and contribute to a broader end, which can be understood as *eudaimonia* – the greatest good of all. As I heard this, I started to reflect upon how my prior understanding of happiness seemed to have been thwarted, largely due to the norms of our contemporary modern society, where it is easy to get tricked into believing that happiness should be understood from a hedonic perspective (i.e. feeling good). Thanks to the eudemonic perspective, I opened up to another view, which helped me see how living a purposeful life might bring a broader sense of fulfillment. In the reality of our everyday lives, we need both these perspectives in order to thrive. This is because hedonia without eudaimonia might contribute to a lot of "empty pleasures," while eudaimonia without hedonia could make our life experiences very "dry."

Astrology and Third-Wave CBT: A Middle Way?

Now that we know a bit more about astrology and different branches of psychology, we might also ask ourselves if there is some middle way. My simple answer is yes, there is. I would like to argue that the concept known as Acceptance and Commitment Therapy (ACT) is equivalent to some crossover in terms of a method that might decrease dysfunction *and* promote well-being simultaneously. This therapeutic framework was created by clinical psychologist Dr Stephen C. Hayes and popularized by medical practitioner, psychotherapist, and psychologist Dr Russ Harris. As I am writing this, I realize how strange this might sound. Are not all methods aimed at reducing psychological distress and dysfunction automatically also aimed at promoting well-being? While that might be true, we need to remind ourselves that traditional psychology has been, and still is, primarily focused on decreasing dysfunction and getting people "back on track" based on our definition and understanding of what it means to be functional according to our societal norms. Based on my experience, people who want to increase or boost their well-being tend not to seek support in psychiatry due to the high demands of people suffering from dysfunction and impaired mental health.

Acceptance and Commitment Therapy (ACT) is an example of a CBT method that originates from behavioral therapy but is considered a "third-wave CBT method" due to its more contextualistic approach.[9] Acceptance and Commitment Therapy is a psychological, evidence-based method with the main focus on increasing *psychological flexibility* – that is, the ability to come in contact with the present moment more fully as a conscious human being while adhering to one's values by either persisting in one's behavior or changing one's behavior so that it serves certain valued ends.[10] In plain English, this means being able to shift perspectives, thoughts, and behaviors so that they fit the current needs of a situation. Psychological flexibility refers to several processes that unfold over time, often defined by how a person adapts to fluctuating situational demands, reconfigures mental resources, shifts perspectives, and balances competing desires, needs, and life domains. Research suggests that flexibility is associated with better mental health and better outcomes in life. On a similar note, we know that a majority of psychopathological diagnoses tend to be associated with

---

[9] Hayes, S. C., Follette, V. M., & Linehan, M. M. (eds). (2004). *Mindfulness and Acceptance: Expanding the cognitive behavioral tradition*. New York: Guilford Press.

[10] Hayes, S. C., Luoma, J. B., Bond, F. W., Masuda, A., & Lillis, J. (2006). Acceptance and commitment therapy: Model, processes and outcomes. *Behaviour Research and Therapy*, *44*(1), 1–25.

rigidity and overall rigid behavior, which contrasts with the state of flexibility.[11]

The Importance of Flexibility when Practicing Astrology

Critics tend to believe that practicing astrology makes people static in their understanding of life. This is often based on the belief that astrology is *deterministic* and that people who practice astrology do so because they want to control or foresee happenings and future events. This could not be further from the truth, according to me. I think the ability to think flexibly is one of the most essential components when practicing astrology, and it also includes asking critical questions, raising concerns, or shifting perspectives if necessary. I believe it is about not letting astrology *define you* but seeing it as something you want to *determine for yourself*. Astrology can help us see the bigger picture, the larger brush-strokes, or the overall themes, but it is up to us to define what actions we want to take based on our free will. The way we interpret and work with our horoscopes is also something that tends to change over time – particularly since our consciousness and awareness tend to expand, resulting in the notion that we can study the same horoscope over decades and still learn to see and interpret it from different angles. Approaching astrology with this mindset makes astrological practice fun and expansive while broadening our minds and behavioral repertoires. Astrologer Steven Forrest once said, "Astrology is the weather report, but you are the weather." Staying flexible and avoiding becoming dogmatic or deterministic when practicing astrology may be challenging, as the urge to "know it all" or "be in control of one's destiny"

[11] Kashdan, T. B., & Rottenberg, J. (2010). Psychological flexibility as a fundamental aspect of health. *Clinical Psychology Review*, *30*(7), 865–78.

might take over. Here, we must remember that astrology is a practice of trust and openness.

While some branches of astrology may be more deterministic than others, this book covers personal astrology from a modern, Western perspective and pairs well with maintaining an open approach. I must advocate for flexibility and openness when working with personal charts because if we apply a deterministic approach to a birth chart, we risk becoming static in our understanding of ourselves and our energy. That is why psychological concepts such as flexibility, awareness, and increasing one's agency become important when practicing the kind of astrology I promote. Through openness comes awareness of oneself and, from there, consciousness and acceptance. From acceptance grows self-compassion and the possibility of increasing one's will, trust, and agency.

There also has to be a balance between believing in our agency and trusting that some higher force might guide us. My way of interpreting the astrological phrase "As above, so below" is by making it a reminder that external planetary events are thought to impact us, but there is also potential for *us* to impact the bigger picture through our actions here on Earth. Life might have a greater meaning, but that does not take away the impact we can have on the world through our actions and the narratives we create through our beliefs and actions. Ultimately, it is up to *us* to create meaning from our experiences. In fact, this approach mirrors that of *narrative therapy*, which connects to the astrological practice by exploring personal narratives and life themes.

Astrology: A Form of Narrative Therapy?

Narrative therapy is a therapeutic approach that emphasizes the stories we tell about our lives. It is based on the concept that these narratives shape our identities. The therapy focuses on identifying dominant stories and recognizing prevailing stories that may limit or negatively impact an individual. An important component of narrative therapy is known as *externalization*, which is the process of separating the individual from their issues. This process is somewhat similar to *defusion* in the ACT framework, and can help reduce the impact of problems by viewing them as external rather than inherent parts of oneself. Linking this to astrology, astrological practice is well-suited to help externalize life events. We can work with our natal horoscope as a mirror from which we can reflect upon our life story, externalize, and find space between ourselves and the events in our lives. That is also why I claim that astrology is suitable for reflection on how societal norms impact us daily, simply because the more deterministic approach to astrology suggests that there is some innate essence available in all of us which we can activate and nurture throughout life. However, it is essential to mention that just as with narrative therapy, astrology should not be used to blame external circumstances. We do not blame the planets or our horoscopes for our lives, choices, or behaviors. Instead, astrology can function as a tool to re-author narratives by reflecting upon the planetary energies and creating alternative stories that align more closely with our desired expression. This can even be seen as a way to transform planetary energies by working with planetary energies and astrology; this way, we could help bring empowerment and change. Both narrative therapy and astrology are similar in that sense. However, narrative therapy uses dialogue and reflection to challenge and change life narratives. In contrast, astrology uses the positions of celestial bodies as a reflective tool to understand life patterns and possibilities. While narrative therapy is a scientifically grounded approach focusing on psychological change, decoding a horoscope is a more metaphysical process grounded in symbolism and reflection rather than scientific evidence. Both offer valuable insights into personal development by emphasizing the power of personal narratives and the potential for self-discovery and transformation.

The Importance of Ethics

Now that we have explored how astrology and psychology align and differ from each other, we have reached the important subject of *ethics*. Although briefly discussed at the beginning of this chapter, we will now take a deeper look at how to maintain an ethical approach to astrology through the help of concrete ethical guidelines. From a broader perspective, we could even say that practicing ethical astrology is a question of *sustainability*. Most of us might think of sustainability as linked to environmental causes. Although it is, in fact, about promoting a healthy environment, we must remember that a healthy environment cannot exist without thriving humans, societies, and economies.

From an *ethical and environmental* point of view, astrology is relatively benign. It does not rely on exploiting natural resources or producing significant waste. However, astrology's impact on individuals' mental health and well-being can be mixed. For some, it can offer comfort, insight, and a sense of agency. For others, overreliance on astrological predictions might lead to anxiety or decision-making that ignores practical realities. Astrology could also make us more self-centered if we forget to apply a holistic approach when interpreting our experiences. I know I have mentioned it earlier, but this needs to be emphasized: Astrology is about finding ourselves in the larger scheme of things. "As above, so below" — by acknowledging that we are, in fact, part of something greater!

Conclusively, sustainability is related to astrology and is closely linked to ethics depending on how humans engage with it — whether we use it to complement other perspectives or rely on it *exclusively*. What do we *do* with it? Are we causing harm or trying to contribute to increased sustainability through well-being? By taking a systems approach and acknowledging how specific issues interconnect, we can avoid promoting unsustainable habits that could harm our sustainability, related to our mental health, overconsumption, social injustice, and so on. That is why complementary perspectives could be critical, such as awareness around *ethics, psychology, philosophy,* and *sociology*. Astrology has shown remarkable adaptability, moving from ancient traditions to digital platforms. Let us invite it to grow while we aim for a more sustainable society. More concretely, we can foster an ethical approach to our astrological practice through the four guidelines listed below – whether our practice is meant only for ourselves or in relation to working with a client.

Ethical Guidelines

1. *Aim to be helpful and not cause any harm through astrological practice.*

Engaging in ethical behavior and being helpful to avoid causing harm should be a commendable approach and a fundamental principle of astrological practice. This mindset includes a genuine concern for the well-being of others while fostering positive relationships built on trust and respect. Many contextual factors, such as inequality, norms, conventions, and societal hierarchies, tend to influence us and not always work in favor of our highest good. These contextual factors do not just disappear as we start engaging with astrology. By aiming to be helpful and intending not to cause harm, our astrological practice can function as a room where we can be invited to rest from all that society imposes on us while also spreading a message of empathy, compassion, hope, and growth. But what happens if we *unwillingly* cause harm despite following ethical codes of conduct? First, daring to talk about this subject is essential. People can have the best intentions yet still cause *unintentional harm*. One way I work with this is always to set an intention of what we are striving to achieve. This intention can favorably be shared with the client, and the client is encouraged to share any feedback on how the information landed while being communicated. Words are powerful, so I begin every session by stating something similar to "I am here today to guide you based on my best capacity. I intend to guide you in an empathic, compassionate way where we work together to gain clarity and create a safe space where you feel welcome to express yourself fully." As astrologers, we must be open to *feedback* and acknowledge if we have caused unintentional harm. With that also comes the notion that all of us will probably go through the process of having caused unintentional harm sometime during our astrological career despite following rigorous ethical guidelines and doing our best. Openness is the antidote to any harmful interactions – and this goes both ways. An example of what might be considered a *harmful interaction* is retrieved from a real-life incident. A client of mine came to me for a consultation after experiencing what she called "a horrible astrology consultation." Before I give this example, I want to be clear that I am not sharing this with the intention of looking down upon other astrologers and their way of practicing astrology. Instead, I want to raise this as an example of how small comments can cause great harm when delivered unethically.

The client was born with Jupiter conjunct her Ascendant. For those who do not know astrology, the Ascendant is associated with our physical appearance, and Jupiter tends to expand all it touches. The astrologer identified this placement and commented on the client's body size, insinuating she might have problems shedding extra pounds and maintaining a healthy weight. In addition, the astrologer also made a joke about the client needing to "keep a lock on her fridge." As a psychologist, I get frustrated and sad when I hear these examples. We know that the norms in our society tend to be very harsh on us about how our bodies look, particularly for women in the Western world, and that is why we need to be aware of *harmful societal norms* influencing our practice. We must strive to create that safe space to limit the reproduction of harmful norms and ideas. To clarify, I am not against discussing body image or the client's relation to their body during the astrological consultation. However, we must acknowledge the norms around the body, especially in relation to women, and open those subjects with empathy, compassion, and respect. What this astrologer did not know was that this client had struggled with accepting her body for almost all her life, so this comment triggered a lot of sadness and anxiety and left her with an uneasy feeling. In my opinion, a better way to talk about the Jupiter conjunct Ascendant placement in relation to body image could have been through an open question such as "How do you relate to your body?" and from there, let the client set the tone for how the conversation should develop.

2. *Honor the independence and self-governance of individuals who seek astrological guidance.*

Honoring the independence and self-governance of individuals who seek guidance through astrology is crucial for fostering a sense of *empowerment* and *self-awareness*. I always say, "I am not here to tell you who you are or what you should do because you know that already — I am simply providing you with a complementary perspective." Astrology is a tool many people turn to as a way to gain insights into their lives. Knowing this, we need to respect the client's autonomy to explore life without judgment while promoting a culture of open-mindedness and inclusivity. Again, this is also directly related to contextual factors in our society as we have all grown up in societal systems that somehow have impacted us and often have had us questioning or diminishing our ability or agency. Each person's life journey is *unique*, and by honoring the client's independence, we can create a space where diverse beliefs and practices can coexist harmoniously. Accepting individual autonomy encourages personal growth and self-discovery, leading to a more fulfilling and enriched life experience. An example of how to practically incorporate this guideline is by being aware that the perspective brought by astrology is merely an *addition* to what the client *already knows*. A constructive way to do so is, for example, by stating a disclaimer before beginning the consultation. This disclaimer could be phrased like this: "I am here today to offer you my astrological insights, but I want to remind you that you are your best expert, and my guidance is simply an additional perspective to what you already know." Additionally, we could continue by saying, "It is also important for me to tell you, before beginning this session, that you can take whatever advice resonates with you and leave whatever doesn't, because this session is aimed to increase your agency and leave you with a sense of empowerment."

"But what about giving the client constructive advice?" you might ask. Is that not something that could impose the client's own agency? Well, of course, we need to provide some guidance because that is at the core of astrological practice. However, *how* we say something is just as important as *what* we say, if not more important. Let me take another example — this time from a consultation where I consulted an astrologer for guidance. I had just come out of a problematic period of secondary infertility and had experienced many consecutive miscarriages when aiming to have my second child. It was my fourth pregnancy, and at the time of the consultation I was still in the early stage of the pregnancy, where everything felt fragile. I went to a highly renowned astrologer for overall life guidance. I was interested in doing something for myself that might give me back some hope and power and push me in a positive direction after having gone through so many hardships related to my health and fertility. During the consultation, the astrologer delivered many valuable insights. But as he started talking about the *future* and *children,* my nervous system got activated, and I remember feeling uneasy. I am not against talking about children or pregnancies during an astrological consultation, but I am very *aware* that these topics can be sensitive to some — in particular because we know that many people tend to struggle with unexplained infertility, while others may not want to have kids despite societal norms perhaps pushing us to believe we should. During my session, the astrologer, unsolicited, said: "I see two children in your life." I immediately responded that I had always thought I would have three.

His response: "No way! You are not here to have many children; you are here to be a teacher for the world — the world is your children." Without giving me room to respond, he continued: "Next year could be a good year to get pregnant." I answered that I was, in fact, in early pregnancy now, again, after having gone through three consecutive miscarriages, where one was a missed spontaneous abortion in week 13. He continued by saying, "Okay, so *if* this pregnancy works out for you, it will be a girl, and this pregnancy will then be your *last,* and you should tell your husband to get a *vasectomy.*" I was baffled. Not only because I do not like to be told what to do or how things will be, but also because of his lack of compassion considering everything I had just shared. Wait, what? My partner should get a vasectomy, and if this pregnancy works out, then it will be my last? I was in shock, and the consultation did not give me the expected boost I had anticipated.

In retrospect, I can see that my *agency* was overlooked while *my voice* and *experience* were diminished in favor of *his interpretations.* This is also an excellent example of how unawareness about power imbalances can influence how we feel during an astrological consultation. In this case, this renowned astrologer was highly unaware of his impact on my life and, ultimately, failed to notice how his guidance affected my mental health. To cut a long story short, the pregnancy did work out, and I gave birth to a healthy daughter. Nevertheless, I cannot stop wondering why it seemed so important for him to phrase the information so confidently. There is a fine line between proving yourself and your astrological skills and also leaving room for the client to explore life from their perspective. A more ethical way this astrologer could have approached me would have been through asking an open question such as "Have you thought about having more children?" and then allowing me to elaborate from my point of view before giving me "the answers." That would have allowed me to feel more empowered and exercise my agency. Ultimately, as an astrologer, I see no point in telling people *exactly* what their life is going to look like according to astrology — because I believe that can ultimately create more harm than good, in particular since astrology is *not* equivalent to an exact science where such detailed information can be uttered with such certainty. Nobody knows the mysteries of life. This is also important when we read our horoscopes for ourselves — the notion that astrology can provide the larger brush-strokes and help us reflect, but that the art of astrology tends to include asking the *right questions* rather than finding the *"right answers."*

3. Uphold professional confidentiality and anonymity in astrological interactions unless there is a risk of causing serious harm by remaining silent.

Confidentiality is a crucial aspect of the therapist-client relationship, and this also applies to the astrological setting. Confidentiality is the obligation to keep all information clients share during sessions private and secure. This helps create a safe and trusting environment where clients feel comfortable discussing their thoughts, feelings, and experiences without fear of judgment or disclosure to others. This might seem obvious when we think about going to a therapist or a psychologist, where we might be invited to share intimate details about ourselves and our life experiences – but what about confidentiality within the astrological context? Is it evident that confidentiality should be applied also in the *astrological setting*? Perhaps not. There are currently no formal rules or regulations ensuring that astrologers maintain confidentiality regarding their clients, which emphasizes the need for us to highlight this topic when striving to practice astrology ethically. In the therapeutic setting, psychologists and psychiatrists keep track of a patient's history and progress with the help of psychiatric records. From my point of view, a psychiatric record can somewhat mirror similar information found in a horoscope (minus the medical or diagnostic information). The same themes that emerge during a therapeutic session with a psychologist may also be discussed when meeting an astrologer. The fact that a horoscope can reveal so much information about a person's life is something we must consider with care and respect. I always say that opening a client's horoscope reminds me of when I used to open psychiatric records at my former job as a psychologist – only that the horoscope somehow invites me to look beyond the implications of societal norms. It is crucial to establish safety when initiating a session, and therefore it is a good idea to tell the client perhaps that "during this session, all that is shared will stay here in this room." When individuals feel assured that their personal information will be kept private and secure, they are more likely to seek help without fear of judgment or repercussions. In healthcare, for example, patients are more willing to disclose sensitive information to their healthcare providers if they trust it will remain confidential. Confidentiality builds trust and fosters a safe environment for individuals to seek guidance and support without fearing that their privacy may be compromised.

4. Do not use others' birth data without explicit consent unless it is already publicly available.

When using birth data for astrological purposes, respecting individuals' privacy and seeking consent before accessing or utilizing their personal information is essential. Again, let us refer back to the therapeutic setting and compare a horoscope to psychiatric (or medical) records. Opening up the records of patients whom we do not treat is strictly forbidden in a medical or therapeutic setting. Some systems ensure logging of what documents have been opened, by whom, what information has been retrieved, and why. Although a birth chart might seem *less sensitive* than a psychiatric record, we must take this guideline seriously. A horoscope holds an immense amount of information and should be handled accordingly. Therefore, asking for consent before using someone's birth data demonstrates respect for the individual's autonomy and ensures that they are comfortable with how their information is being used. It also promotes transparency and trust between the astrologer and the individual seeking insights into their astrological chart. By prioritizing consent in the astrological practice, we can uphold ethical standards, honor individuals' rights to privacy, and create a safe and respectful space for exploring ourselves and our experiences.

An example of when we might come in contact with this in real life is if we meet a client for a consultation and the client asks, "But wait, do you mind just checking something about my husband?" Such a question might seem harmless at first glance, but this is precisely when we must pause and reflect on our ethical obligations. I write this because this is not an uncommon question, and some astrologers might be okay with opening up the client's husband's horoscope and providing some insight. However, I am not okay with it, and this is simply because, without the consent of that third person, I believe it is not ethical to open the horoscope or deliver any interpretations.

The same goes for people who post anonymous charts in social media communities without the owner of that chart being aware. The only exception here is perhaps regarding children. While I believe children's horoscopes should be interpreted with *even more* care than those of adults, if a parent seeks astrological guidance and wants to ask about their child's horoscope, I would say it is okay. We must believe that a parent has the best intentions for their child. However, as soon as the child reaches a certain level of maturity (perhaps around 13 years of age?) and they are ready to understand the implications related to an astrology consultation, I believe the most ethical thing to do is to involve the child and ask whether they give their consent or not to have their horoscope read.

Communicate without false expectations or definitive statements, acknowledging that astrological markers can manifest in diverse ways. When practicing astrology, it is essential to approach it with a critical mindset to avoid false expectations or taking definitive statements too seriously. This might sound strange coming from an astrologer – I mean, aren't we the ones who are thought to be able to look into the future and tell what will happen? Perhaps not quite like that, as I have tried to explain.

While astrology can provide guidance and spark self-reflection, it is essential to remember that it is not a science and should not be used as the sole basis for making important life decisions. I believe it is a helpful tool for self-discovery and should be used to identify the larger brush-strokes rather than a set of strict rules or predictions. Similarly, each person's interpretation of their astrological chart can vary over their lifespan, and it is crucial to maintain skepticism and open-mindedness simultaneously. "How do we do that?" one might ask. First, it is essential to keep an open mind and acknowledge the limitations of astrology; second, enjoy its benefits without relying too heavily on it or setting unrealistic expectations. I firmly believe that astrological practice can also become more fun if we see it as an explorative practice rather than a tool to figure out "the truth."

I am aware that some schools of astrology might be more "rigid" or deterministic than others, which is fine. However, when we deal with individuals, we need to be aware of the *harm* we could cause by speaking in *absolutes*. The saying "The only thing that is constant is change" makes a lot of sense and applies to our work in astrology. Instead of being dogmatic, we can focus on becoming more open – at least, that is how I want to practice astrology. At the same time, it is crucial not to provide clients with false hope. Oh, what a balancing act!

An example is if a client is going through a challenging astrological transit (e.g. Saturn conjunct the Moon, or Pluto squaring the Sun). In such a situation, it is essential to *acknowledge* the potential hardships that may come with such transits and, at the same time, work with increasing *agency, acceptance,* and *hope*. I am a firm believer that several perspectives can exist simultaneously, and this is something that I want to permeate my astrological practice and inspire others to follow as well. Understand the limits of astrological knowledge and the boundaries related to the astrological practice, and direct individuals elsewhere when their requirements exceed our expertise.

While many people find *comfort, guidance,* and *insight* through astrology, it is also essential to understand that it is not a one-size-fits-all solution for every aspect of life. Some individuals may seek astrological guidance for decisions better addressed by other professionals, such as medical doctors, psychologists, financial advisors, or career counselors. This is also when we, as astrologers, need to be confident enough to know our limitations. In particular, astrology is a broad subject with multiple orientations and uses. In personal astrology, we focus on *guiding people* – but that does not mean that the practice is specifically or solely aimed at advice related to, for example, *personal finances*. There are financial astrologers for that, and if we want, we can also go to astrologers specializing in fertility, physical health, or relationship dynamics. It is vital, first of all, to be clear about what kind of guidance we offer in our astrological practice. Secondly, it is also crucial to refer clients elsewhere if we believe they might be better guided by somebody else.

An example is how some clients are curious and want to ask questions about fertility. In those situations, I always answer that "pregnancy and fertility are outside of my scope, but I can direct you to an astrologer who has that expertise – or I can suggest you seek guidance from a medical doctor who specializes in fertility." Being clear about what we do and don't do is essential to provide clarity. It can also help us establish a sense of safety for our clients. Having clear boundaries is a sign of professionalism. I also believe it is important to communicate these boundaries beforehand so the client knows what to expect before booking a consultation. Another example of when we might need to refer clients to seek other advice is if we are dealing with potential *medical issues* or mental health issues. This even applies to people with adequate academic training, like me. I believe it would be highly unethical for me to treat someone's anxiety based on astrology, simply because the role of an astrologer is not to diagnose or treat neuropsychiatric variations. That is why I have tried to be clear that I do not treat or diagnose any psychopathology when practicing astrology.

Both clients and practitioners must recognize these boundaries and understand that astrology can complement, but not replace, other forms of support and expertise. By acknowledging the limitations of astrological practice and knowing when to direct clients elsewhere, we can uphold our ethical standards and ensure that clients receive the most appropriate help for their needs.

Chapter 2

The Horoscope: Your Unique Life Compass

What Is a Horoscope?

I began this book by explaining that astrology is more than generalized Sun sign interpretations and that the horoscope is more than the astrological columns we read in magazines. A horoscope is, in fact, *a map* and a snapshot of the sky around Earth during an exact moment. For some, seeing a horoscope for the first time might be overwhelming — at least, that is how it was for me. All those symbols, glyphs, and lines made me curious but also very overwhelmed. *Where do I begin? How do I decode all this information?*

Learning astrology is complex but does not have to be complicated. I usually start by explaining the four main components: *planets, zodiac signs, houses,* and *aspects.*

In a horoscope, *planets* represent archetypes or, plainly put, *energies* that express themselves through *zodiac signs.* These energies (planets) are projected (in zodiac signs) through you and into the outside world via the astrological *houses* (i.e. the 12 "sections" drawn up in the horoscope). Lastly, *aspects* provide information about the *relationships* between energies (planets in zodiac signs) in your horoscope and symbolize how the energies relate to and work with each other. This book will teach you how to use planets, zodiac signs, and houses to start making interpretations and connecting your interpretations to modern psychological concepts of well-being. Therefore, the scope of this book is limited to giving you a basic understanding of the *planets,* the *zodiac signs,* and the *houses.* Aspects are equally important but not necessary when starting to make interpretations. Starting off at a very basic level can be a good idea, limiting oneself to understanding how to interpret a planet in a sign in a house before incorporating the aspects. That is what we will learn in this book.

What Kind of Astrology?

Before we examine the 12 astrological houses in more detail, it is essential to state what kind of astrology this book is based upon. As mentioned, there are many branches of astrology, and some use different methods to calculate the distribution of houses. In astrology, the methods we use to draw a horoscope are called *house systems*. In the old days, drawing a horoscope was done by hand and required in-depth knowledge of astronomy, geometry, and mathematics. Thanks to our modern technological advancements, we now have apps and websites that help us with this. Because of this, exploring and trying different kinds of house systems is also easier. In this book, we will work with the house system known as Placidus, which is one of modern astrology's most widely used house systems.

Generally, the discussion of what house system to use or what house system is "the best" can cause confusion and frustration among astrological practitioners. This is because the way we calculate and draw up the houses will impact how a horoscope looks and how the planets will be distributed, ultimately impacting interpretation. Without going too far into this subject, I want to highlight that houses are a *human invention*, meaning that the sky around the Earth is not divided into different sections in its natural state. Therefore, house systems are simply a way for humans to identify planetary energies and their position in relation to the Earth and, from there, bring forth an interpretation. Due to this, the same horoscope can sometimes look a bit different depending on the house system we used to calculate the chart. This is nothing to worry about or pay too much attention to at this stage, and the question of what house system is "the best" is beyond the scope of this book. However, I do recommend learning *one* house system at a time by thoroughly getting to know that system before changing to another.

I think about different house systems in a similar way to how I see different types of tarot decks or how I think of the difference between a tarot deck and an oracle card deck. We can receive information through both; it is merely a matter of preferences, as some people might be drawn to working with oracle cards, while others might prefer tarot cards. I like using the house system known as Placidus when practicing astrology. Despite this, I have also attended workshops where the astrologer has interpreted charts using other systems, such as Whole Signs. That works fine for me, but I recommend using other systems only when you have gotten further along in your astrological practice, as it might otherwise cause confusion based on the fact that there are, in fact, some interpretative differences, as well as differences in terms of how the planets might be distributed within the chart.

Another important thing is that most horoscopes are *geocentric,* meaning that we imagine the Earth in the middle of our map of the sky. This contrasts with the scientific view, where we think about our solar system as *heliocentric,* with the Sun in the center. Most ways of practicing astrology are based on a geocentric perspective simply because this allows us to study the sky from our position on Earth. This book will base its understanding and interpretations on the astrological branch known as *Western tropical astrology*. "Western" contrasts with Eastern traditions such as Vedic astrology. "Tropical" refers to the position of the Earth *relative to the Sun and the seasons* rather than the *actual positions* of the constellations (zodiac signs) in the sky. Some people are surprised when I tell them that the planetary positions in zodiac signs, as seen through the lens of Western tropical astrology, differ from what astronomers observe when they identify planets and their actual physical positions in the sky.

This is due to a phenomenon known as *precession*, which is the gradual wobble of Earth's rotational axis, which causes the positions of the stars and constellations to shift over a cycle of approximately 26,000 years. This phenomenon leads to a divergence between the astrological and astronomical observations and tends to be a top argument used by critics when they state why astrology should be "falsified." Among astronomers, precession is often accounted for to ensure that the study of celestial bodies reflects their current positions in the sky, and astronomers tend to adjust their measurements to account for this shift, which affects celestial navigation, calendar systems, and our understanding of the cosmos. In modern Western tropical astrology, precession is not adjusted for or used as a way to understand the planetary positions in the sky. Instead, we use a fixed zodiac system based on the seasons rather than the constellations' current positions. We have fixed points, such as the Vernal Equinox, which to us astrologers are equivalent to the Sun's ingress into the zodiac sign of Aries. Do not worry if you find this complicated, because it is. However, you only need to know that we make a symbolic connection between the zodiac signs and our human experience within Western astrology, grounded in the seasons' cyclical nature rather than the planets' actual positions in the sky. Astrology still works and is fascinating, and precession is nothing we need to pay much attention to, although I think it is important to mention.

A contrasting perspective to *tropical astrology* is known as *sidereal astrology*, which can be explained as being "more aligned" with the physical positions of the planets in the sky. However, as with the house systems, we must remember that both perspectives can provide valuable insights through symbolic interpretation. I think it is essential to be aware of basic knowledge like this when aiming to understand and practice astrology! In conclusion, the kind of astrology used in this book is referred to as Western tropical (geocentric) astrology, and the house system we use is Placidus.

The Horoscope as a Therapeutic Life Compass: Beyond "Strengths and Weaknesses"

Now we have reached the point where we will link the horoscope to the *therapeutic life compass*. Many of us know that astrology is often used for self-reflection and insight into personality traits, strengths, and weaknesses. In this book, we will go beyond that perspective and instead build on the idea that a horoscope can be used just like a life compass to reflect upon one's values and valued life direction. Before learning about the life compass, let us define the difference between *values* and *goals*.

Values and goals are two distinct concepts that play essential roles in guiding our lives. Values refer to principles representing what is meaningful to us — principles that shape our attitudes and behaviors by influencing our decisions and actions in various aspects of life. Goals are specific objectives or targets we aim to achieve within a certain timeframe. Goals are more concrete and measurable than values, as they might help us focus on achieving a specific outcome associated with an end state. While values are the foundation of our beliefs and priorities, goals are the actionable steps we take to manifest those values in our lives. In summary, values are the core principles that guide our choices and define who we are, while goals are more specific and are set to realize our values and aspirations. By aligning our goals with our values, we can create a more meaningful and fulfilling life that reflects what truly matters to us.

Reflecting upon values can be a powerful tool to liberate ourselves from the constraints of societal norms. By taking the time to introspect and identify our core beliefs and principles, we can better understand who we are and what *truly* matters to us. I want to emphasize the word *truly*, as identifying one's values is highly personal, where we might need to contrast ourselves with the norms and break free from what does not fully resonate with us. This self-awareness allows us to question the status quo and evaluate whether the societal expectations we are adhering to align with our authentic selves. Moreover, by aligning our actions with our values, we can live more purposefully and authentically. When we break free from societal norms that may not resonate with us, we open ourselves up to new possibilities and ways of being that are more fulfilling and meaningful. Embracing our values empowers us to make conscious choices, leading to greater fulfillment and inner peace. In this way, reflecting upon values can be a transformative process that enables us to live more authentically and align with what truly matters to us.

One way of coming in contact with our values is by working with a life compass, such as we might use, for example, if we go to a therapist, psychologist, or mental health coach. A life compass is essentially a pie chart or a worksheet representing life themes. This tool aims to help us define a valued direction by stating how we value different life areas and reflecting upon how we think we currently align our actions with those identified values. This tool is commonly used in cognitive behavioral therapies such as Acceptance and Commitment Therapy (ACT) and is often visually represented by a 360-degrees circle illustrating a pie chart of several life areas.

A life compass helps individuals identify their *core values* across various life domains to guide their *actions* and decisions. This model encourages people to live in ways consistent with their personal values, promoting greater psychological flexibility and well-being in areas such as:

- Parenting
- Personal growth

- Leisure
- Spirituality
- Community and environment
- Health
- Social relationships
- Intimate relationships
- Work
- Education

When I refer to the horoscope as a *life compass*, I think of the 12 astrological houses and how the life areas described by the houses correspond to the areas included in the life compass. Before going deeper into this, I want to remind you that this book teaches astrology from a Western tropical perspective, which means that interpretations related to the 12 houses will be made accordingly. The way we will understand the houses in this book differs from how some other astrology schools might interpret them. Having made that clear, let us now move on and see how the horoscope mirrors what psychologists and psychotherapists refer to as a life compass.

I believe that decoding one's horoscope mirrors the process of working with a life compass —at least if we focus on values rather than identifying strengths and weaknesses through our charts, which is how I have chosen to practice astrology. This approach is supported by scientific studies, as exemplified by some researchers who have explored the concept of *life crafting,*[12] which could be described as a structured approach to identifying and pursuing personal goals that align with one's values and aspirations. Key findings from their research suggest that life crafting can significantly enhance an individual's sense of *purpose* and overall *well-being*. This process

[12] Schippers, M. C., & Ziegler, N. (2019). Life crafting as a way to find purpose and meaning in life. *Frontiers in Psychology, 10*(2778). doi: 10.3389/fpsyg.2019.02778

involves reflective exercises that help individuals articulate their goals and aspirations and take practical steps to achieve them. Although this research does not involve astrology, I think working with the horoscope as a life compass could provide a clear sense of direction and contribute to improved personal satisfaction and psychological wellness, mainly since the authors highlight the importance of aligning one's daily activities with broader life goals to foster a meaningful and fulfilling life. The authors summarize their research with the following statement:

> In short, life crafting is about finding out what you stand for (i.e., values and passions), finding out how to make it happen (i.e., goal attainment plans), and telling someone about your plans (i.e., public commitment). Concluding, it seems that life crafting is about taking control of one's life and finding purpose. Based on recent findings, it would be well-advised for many of us to carve out time to do an evidence-based life-crafting intervention.

Based on this, I think that astrology is a useful tool for helping with successful life crafting by using your personal horoscope as your own unique life compass.

Committed Action through Values, Not Goals

As you might have understood, the process of identifying values is closely linked to acting according to those identified values. Without action, there is no change or impact. In the therapeutic setting, taking action in accordance with identified values is sometimes referred to as *committed action*, which has its roots in the ACT model of psychological flexibility and consists of taking active steps in alignment with one's values. Many people tend to set goals, and many of us are used to goal setting as a strategy to commit to action. However, in the ACT model, the term "committed action" is linked to values or valued goals, which tends to be a more personalized approach.

To exemplify this further, goals are often tied to some dichotomy of completion or failure, and an example of a goal could therefore be "I will run 10 kilometers in 50 minutes by next March." The reason or purpose behind such a goal is not expressed, but it clearly defines what is required for the goal to be met and can result in us achieving the goal or not. On the other hand, a value is more qualitative in the sense that it is derived from personal meaning and therefore functions more as a compass than a goal. Why does a person want to run 10 kilometers in 50 minutes by next March? Is it because of a desire to be healthier? If so, that goal could be rephrased and turned into a personal value by defining what makes such a pursuit meaningful.

Reflecting upon our personalized values and defining what to act on also involves detaching ourselves from societal expectations to discover what we value beyond societal norms. Perhaps some of us are under the impression that it is necessary for us to run 10 kilometers in 50 minutes in order to be "healthy." If so, looking at one's values could help us detach ourselves from these preconceptions and also allow for activities that are more in tune with our capacity in the present moment. This way, we can create room to take action in accordance with our desired values purposefully.

Just as we might need complementary perspectives to attain happiness (eudaimonia and hedonia), it is believed that we need both goals and values to feel purpose. The difference is that most of us tend to think about goals when we think about actions or achievements. That is when values can help shift perspectives and allow us to experience more meaning, while also allowing for more flexibility in our everyday behaviors.

Suppose we use astrology sensibly and ethically and combine it with our free will. In that case, it can become an excellent tool to move beyond the fixation on goals and instead let us explore something beyond a linear living model through our values. Since values are not ends or goals, this approach might allow us to experience how everything happens in cycles, illustrated by the astrological practice itself.

The Astrological Life Compass: The 12 Houses

By understanding the energies of each house and their correspondence with life areas, we can use our birth charts to assess where we are and how we might need to adjust and commit to action to better align with our *values*. Merging the framework of the 12 astrological houses with the life areas from the therapeutic life compass provides a structured yet esoteric and unique approach to exploring personal values and finding a direction in life. In the case of empty houses (meaning that the house does not have any planets in it), we can look at the cusp of that house and identify it by zodiac sign (for example, Sagittarius). After that, we identify the ruling planet of that sign (Jupiter) and look at what house Jupiter is in. This simple way of working with empty houses allows us to connect life areas without falling into the trap of "dismissing" certain life areas due to the absence of planets in a particular house.

Let us now explore how each astrological house corresponds to life areas from the therapeutic life compass! As we can see illustrated below, intimate relationships could be linked to the seventh astrological house, while parenting might be related to the fourth or fifth house. Family of origin would be considered a fourth-house theme, and friends, social life, and community are connected to the eleventh house. Health and physical self-care are sixth-house themes, and spirituality could be linked to the twelfth house. Education/learning would be connected to the ninth house, and the tenth house symbolizes work/career. Recreation/leisure is by many considered a fifth-house theme — I think you know what I mean by now!

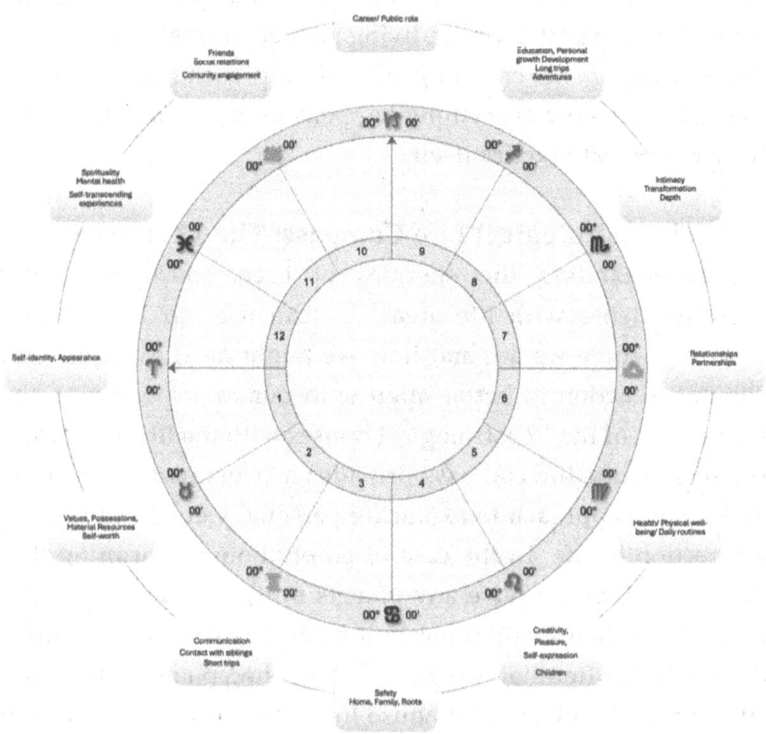

Illustration of how the life areas in the therapeutic life compass correspond to those represented by the 12 astrological houses

Having said this, it becomes clear how all of life's areas can be fitted into the astrological chart via the 12 houses, and decoding one's unique horoscope can be very rewarding in terms of getting in contact with values and interests. The best part is that we can experience *universal guidance* and *spirituality* as the horoscope brings a magical, occult, or esoteric flavor to our therapeutic practice, allowing us to connect with something beyond ourselves.

So, instead of a therapist printing out a sheet of paper where you rate how much you value certain life areas, why not look at your horoscope instead? Not only will you gain insight into yourself and what you appreciate and how, but you will also be able to take part in an esoteric source of human knowledge going back thousands of years, which can help deepen our connection to human history and show us how we are all part of life's cycles through the motions of the planets and the flow of energies.

Now, let us look at each of the 12 houses and how they mirror the life areas of a therapeutic life compass.

The first house: identity

The first house is associated with the sign of Aries and the planet Mars and is often called *the house of personality* or *the house of self*. This area in the birth chart represents personal identity, who we are on a more visible level, our physical appearance, and our most personal traits. The first house is opposed to the seventh house of relationships, emphasizing the relationship to oneself. The first house can help us reflect on what we value regarding our personal identity and external appearance and align our expression of identity with our inner values. By doing so, we can focus on increasing our self-acceptance and self-actualization.

The second house: self-worth, material possessions, and values

The second house is associated with Taurus and the planet Venus. It tends to be called *the house of money* or *values* as it symbolizes our values, monetary or material possessions, self-esteem, and self-worth. The second house can help us reflect upon how we can align ourselves with our values and increase our sense of self-worth by reflecting on our deepest values and relation to material possessions.

The third house: communication

The third house is linked to Gemini and the planet Mercury. It is often called *the house of communication* since it symbolizes our communication (reading, talking, listening) and immediate surroundings. By reflecting upon our values for this life area, we can draw conclusions about what we value on the theme of our communication. How can we nurture our communicative abilities, and what do we value regarding our immediate surroundings? Is there something we would like to learn, or do we want to look at how much and in what way we value communication?

The fourth house: safety, roots, and home environment

The fourth house is connected to the sign of Cancer and the Moon. It is often called *the house of home* and is associated with the most private side of ourselves, our safe base, home, roots, and heritage. This house can help us concretize what we need to feel safe by allowing us to reflect and define what it means to be safe. It can also help us shed light upon values related to family, roots, and our home. What is essential in order to feel safe in a home? What is vital in terms of feeling safe? The fourth house allows us to reflect on inner safety (emotional) and external safety (a home).

The fifth house: creativity, play, and self-expression

The fifth house is often called *the house of children, creativity, self-expression,* and *romance.* It connects to Leo and the Sun and embodies themes such as how to have fun, our childlike expressions of ourselves, our children, and creative pursuits. Working with our values connected to this life area could help us engage in hobbies and activities that bring joy and creativity. It can also help us see what we value regarding leisure activities to better align with what brings us genuine happiness. The fifth house is also about children and could help us reflect upon our childlike nature or our wish to have children.

The sixth house: daily routines and physical health

The sixth house is known as *the house of work and daily routines.* It is connected to the sign Virgo and the planet Mercury and includes areas such as daily work, health, daily routines, and how we serve others daily. By reflecting upon how we value this life area, we can develop healthy routines and habits that reflect our values, well-being, and service to others. In sum, the sixth house is about the structure of everyday life and is excellent for questions regarding how to structure our days and daily routines to better align with our values and promote overall health.

The seventh house: relating to others

The seventh house marks the cusp of the Ascendant and is also the last house below the horizon. It is often called *the house of relationships* as it illuminates intimate, personal relationships or partnerships with another human being. It is connected to the sign of Libra and the planet Venus. By reflecting upon our values connected to the seventh house, we can come in contact with how to cultivate meaningful partnerships that are reciprocal, deeply connected, and aligned with our interpersonal values. This house can help us balance our focus on ourselves (the first house) and on others.

The eighth house: transformation, depth, and intimacy

The eighth house is associated with Scorpio and the planet Pluto. This house is often understood as *the house of death and rebirth*. It includes themes opposite to the second house, such as other people's money or possessions, the transformation of our deep desires and psychological depth, and the death-rebirth process many of us go through when evaluating what we truly desire. When we work with this house in our astrological life compass, embracing life's challenges and changes as opportunities for profound personal transformation is crucial. By identifying what we value in intimacy, we can align our actions within this area to better reflect our values and desires.

The ninth house: development, education, and travel

The ninth house is opposite the third house and tends to be referred to as *the house of long journeys*. The ninth house opposes the third house of communication and our immediate surroundings. The knowledge attained through communication (third house) can be transformed and put into meaning via the ninth house. It is connected with Sagittarius and the planet Jupiter and includes themes such as higher learning, foreign travel, expansion, and the creation of higher meaning. By reflecting upon how we relate to themes like meaning, expansion, education, or travel, we can explore philosophical beliefs and educational opportunities and expand our worldview and spiritual understanding.

The tenth house: career and public role

The tenth house is associated with Capricorn and the planet Saturn and is often called *the house of career*. It opposes the fourth house, which symbolizes themes related to our roots and the most safe and private side of ourselves. Based on this, the tenth house symbolizes our most public role and our mark on this world. By studying the tenth house in your horoscope, you can come closer to how you relate to and what you value about a career, and align your values with your actions to take tangible steps towards a career path that brings professional success and fulfills your aspirations and values.

The eleventh house: friends, community, and societal causes

The eleventh house opposes the fifth house for self-expression and is often called *the house of a social community*. It is associated with the sign Aquarius and the planet Uranus and embodies themes such as social community, groups of friends, the future, social causes, and progressive pursuits. Working with the eleventh house teaches us what we value regarding engaging with communities and friends. Through reflection, we can move closer to aligning ourselves with community groups and friendships that support our aspirations and reflect our ideals and hopes for the future.

The twelfth house: spirituality and mysticism

The twelfth house is connected with the sign of Pisces and the planet Neptune and is often referred to as *the house of solitude, the house of spirituality,* or *the house of universal consciousness.* It also rules our compassion for people who need help and understanding. It opposes the sixth house of our daily routines and habits, which makes the interpretation of this house more inclined towards dreams and experiences different from our daily tasks and everyday life. If the sixth house is the day, then the twelfth house is the dream. Reflecting upon your values related to the twelfth house can help you navigate the importance of spending time in introspection and solitude. How do you value your connection to the Universe? To mystical experiences? To being of service by helping those less fortunate? By exploring the twelfth house and identifying your values, you can decide whether spirituality, mysticism, and self-transcending causes are something you want to make room for in your life, and if so, how.

Chapter 3

The Planets and the Promotion of Well-Being

We have finally reached the stage where we will start exploring how to work with the planetary archetypes and connect them to modern psychology through reflective questions. We will connect the planets (energies) to modern psychological concepts and bridge the evidence with the esoteric. An important thing to mention is that the interpretations below are merely suggestions intended to be used as a basis for self-reflection to get in contact with one's values. Remember that this book covers integrating psychology and astrology through the lens of flexible exploration of personal values rather than the more static approach of "strengths and weaknesses" related to planets in signs.

Introducing the Planets

Before we connect the planets to these psychological concepts, we must first briefly define the planets' role in astrology. To put this simply, planets can be understood as energies. In astrology, there are four essential components: planets, signs, houses, and aspects. Planets (energies) express themselves through zodiac signs. These energies (planets) are projected through you and into the outside world via the astrological houses. The aspects can provide information about the relationships between the energies (planets) in your birth chart and symbolize how the energies within you relate to and work with each other. In this book, we will not make interpretations based on aspects. Instead, we will limit our practice to focusing on planets in signs in houses and make accurate reflective interpretations.

Planets are archetypal energies, and different zodiac signs rule these. According to this perspective, we can see the zodiac signs as different costumes or lenses through which the energies express themselves. Knowing this, we can understand that some costumes (signs) might fit slightly better for some planets than others, keeping in mind that the signs are, in fact, first and foremost, just different clothes that allow the energies (planets) to take on various expressions. In theory, there is a concept known as essential dignities or planetary dignity and debility, which highlights and suggests that planets can be *exalted* (extra strong) in some signs, as well as *in domicile* (in the sign it rules), and *in detriment* (functioning differently, often not according to its potential). A planet in detriment is placed in a sign opposite the sign it rules. In contrast, an astrological fall involves the planet being in the sign positioned directly opposite its sign of exaltation. I want to be clear that my teachings of modern astrology do not include the notion that a planet in a sign of domicile or exaltation (i.e. in a costume it was fitted for) is "better" than a planet in a sign where it experiences its exile or fall (i.e. a costume with slightly "worse fit"). Instead, we can approach this concept from the point of view of resources rather than as "good" or "bad." A planet is not better or worse because it is in a particular sign. However, there will be different expressions, just as we might express ourselves differently depending on whether we wear pajamas, sport clothes or a suit.

Let us now move on to exploring the planets further by imagining ourselves on a journey through the solar system. We can see how the astrological phrase "As above, so below" is embodied through the energies (planets) that make up our existence. We begin at the center of our solar system by looking at our most central luminary – the Sun. From there, we move outwards to Pluto as we discover the archetypal energies of the planets and how they are connected to our human experience.

Personal versus Collective Planets

In modern astrology, planets are categorized based on how long it takes for them to orbit around the Sun, ultimately influencing their impact and astrological interpretation. This distinction separates them into "personal" and "collective/generational" planets. Personal planets include the Sun, Moon, Mercury, Venus, and Mars. These planets move more quickly through the zodiac, affecting individual personality traits and day-to-day experiences to a more considerable extent. Their influences are more immediate and personal because they change signs relatively quickly, reflecting individual moods, behaviors, and habits. This is also why people born with the same Sun sign can be very different from each other and have very different charts. Celestial bodies like the Moon change signs every two to three days, meaning that people born with the same Sun sign (identity) can have different Moon signs (emotionality). The Sun, Moon, Mercury, Venus, and Mars are considered personal because they directly impact individual characteristics and are prominent in shaping one's personal astrology.

Collective or generational planets include Jupiter, Saturn, Uranus, Neptune, and Pluto. These planets move slowly, staying in each zodiac sign for several years. They shape broader social movements, generational themes, and long-term societal transformations. The distinction between personal and collective planets in astrology reflects the scope of their influence – from the deeply personal aspects shaped by the faster-moving planets to the broad, societal trends influenced by the slow-moving planets. This categorization helps astrologers understand and interpret planets' varying impacts on individual lives and connect them to larger generational themes.

The Personal Planets

The Sun: Self-Actualization

Let us begin with the Sun, which, like its position in the solar system, reflects the most central part of ourselves — the identity, the Self, who we grow into being on a *conscious* level, our life-force energy, and how we radiate our energy. The Sun is the body of light that gives life to our existence, and without the Sun we would not survive, and all other planets revolve around the Sun. Through that, we realize how vital this luminary is for our understanding of the expression of a coherent identity and sense of self.

Before moving on to explore how the planetary energy of the Sun can be mirrored by modern psychology, let us first take a look at how other astrologers have defined the Sun's function. April Elliott Kent[13] describes the Sun as "your inner superstar" and "the outward style of your inner hero." She continues by stating that the Sun represents identity, and what makes you *you*. According to April, we can understand the Sun as symbolic of confidence and related to concepts such as self, life goals, ego, and charisma. Astrologer Steven Forrest[14] defines the Sun as "the development of a coherent, operational self-image" and "the focusing of one's willpower and capacity of positive action" as well as "the creation of ego." He continues by stating some key questions related to the Sun, such as: "Who am I?" "What kinds of experiences help me strengthen and clarify my self-image?" "Where can I find and expand my personal power?" and "What unconscious biases shape my view of the world?"

---

[13] Kent, A. E. (2011). *The Essential Guide to Practical Astrology*. New York: Alpha Books/ Penguin.

[14] Forrest, S. (1988). *The Inner Sky*. Borrego Springs, CA: Seven Paws Press.

Based on my interpretation, the energy of the Sun would mirror the psychological concept known as *self-actualization,* which focuses on becoming and expressing one's true self, emphasizing the importance of personal integrity, *authenticity,* and fulfilling one's unique potential. These principles drive individuals towards embracing their *true nature* by fulfilling their potential and shining brightly in their personal and professional lives. This alignment shows how both a psychological and an astrological perspective can provide valuable insights into personal growth and fulfillment. "Self-actualization" is a term coined by Abraham Maslow which refers to realizing or fulfilling one's talents and potentialities. It is the process of becoming more fully oneself, the person one is inherently "meant to be." This process includes harnessing one's abilities and making meaningful achievements that resonate with one's true self.

So, if the Sun reflects a person's individual journey towards becoming self-actualized, the Sun's position in a birth chart can help us reflect upon finding a valued life direction where we allow ourselves to take conscious action towards self-actualization according to our identified values. Astrologically, the Sun drives one's primary motivation and will and represents a person's basic identity, the conscious mind's potential, and the ability to assert personal power. The Sun encourages independence, urging one to act from personal convictions rather than conforming to external pressures. By incorporating what we know about self-actualization, let us now rephrase one of Steven Forrest's questions by asking the following:

> "What kind of values do I want to act upon in order to strengthen and clarify my identity through self-actualization?"

Self-Actualization and Well-Being

Maslow[15] highlighted the relationship between self-actualization and well-being, although he used the terms "self-actualization" or "full-humanness" rather than the term "well-being." In recent years, modern researchers have confirmed this connection by linking self-actualization to multiple aspects of well-being, such as life satisfaction, self-acceptance, positive relations, personal growth, autonomy, environmental mastery, and purpose.[16] It is also interesting how studies like this link Maslow's idea[17] that self-actualized individuals actually report higher levels of self-transcendence (i.e. the ability to go beyond their ego and self and instead unite in self-transcending pursuits that connect them to humanity as a whole) by connecting self-actualization with the unity aspect of the self-transcendent experience, without any "loss of self." In simple terms, this means that self-actualizing individuals seem to be able to paradoxically merge with a common humanity while also maintaining a strong identity and sense of self. Knowing this, we can understand that working on ourselves and expressing our identity does not have to contradict our will to transcend ourselves in pursuits to help humanity as a whole. You can read more about the concept of self-transcendence in relation to Neptune.

[15] Maslow, A. H. (1998). *Toward a Psychology of Being* (3rd edn). New York: Wiley. (Original work published in 1962.)

[16] Kaufman, S. B. (2023). Self-actualizing people in the 21st century: Integration with contemporary theory and research on personality and well-being. *Journal of Humanistic Psychology, 63*(1), 51–83.

[17] Maslow, A. H. (1971). *The Farther Reaches of Human Nature.* New York: Penguin.

Enhance Well-Being through Self-Actualization: The Sun through the Signs

Sun in Aries

The Sun in Aries brings dynamic energy that is assertive, pioneering, and enthusiastic. This fire sign is known for its desire to initiate action, embrace challenges, and assert independence. When considering how to navigate values and practically express the energy of the Sun in Aries to increase well-being through self-actualization, reflecting upon themes like bravery, independence, and leadership could be useful. Below are some reflection questions that can be used to reflect upon values related to the process of self-actualization inspired by the Sun in Aries:

- What are your passions, and how do you cultivate the courage to pursue opportunities that align with your true passions?
- Do you value initiating new projects or goals that resonate deeply with your personal desires?
- Do you find it valuable to set and work towards personal goals independently?
- Do you seek out challenges that stretch your capabilities and allow you to grow? How important is that to you?
- To what extent do you value taking on leadership roles or opportunities that allow you to influence and motivate others?

Sun in Taurus

Utilizing the energy of the Sun in Taurus to promote well-being through self-actualization could include grounding yourself in stability and engaging deeply with the physical and sensual aspects of life. By valuing a solid foundation, exercising patience, and appreciating the sensory world, you can create an environment conducive to growth. The Sun in Taurus brings energies of stability, persistence, and appreciation for the finer things in life. Taurus is an earth sign known for its practical determination, and a strong desire for security and comfort. Harnessing the characteristics of the Sun in Taurus involves reflecting upon one's values related to stability, sensory experiences, and gradual but consistent progress. Below are some reflection questions that can be used to reflect upon values related to the process of self-actualization inspired by the Sun in Taurus.

- To what extent do you value sensory experiences such as gardening, cooking, or other activities that allow you to explore yourself by using your senses? And how do you incorporate them and express them in your daily life?
- Do you value your resilience and determination as a personal strength?
- How do you relate to patience in achieving your personal goals?
- How do you value and incorporate long-term goals and appreciation for the small steps along the way?
- What activities do you find valuable for nurturing your self-worth and sense of beauty?

Sun in Gemini

The Sun in Gemini brings qualities of adaptability, communication, and curiosity. Gemini is an air sign linked to intellectual exploration, social interaction, and the exchange of ideas. Working with the Sun in Gemini to promote well-being through self-actualization involves tapping into the sign's love for learning, communication, and social interaction. Embracing intellectual growth, enhancing communicative abilities, and fostering adaptability serve the broader goals of personal development and self-actualization. Below are some reflection questions that can be used to reflect upon values related to the process of self-actualization inspired by the Sun in Gemini.

- To what extent do you value gathering information and learning new things?
- Do you express your natural curiosity?
- Do you relate to continual intellectual growth as a core aspect of self-actualization? If so, how do you express that through your identity?
- How do you value social interaction?
- Do you believe flexibility is an important trait for personal growth and self-actualization? If so, how do you incorporate that into your daily life?

Sun in Cancer

The Sun in Cancer brings energies of sensitivity, emotional depth, and nurturing. Cancer is a water sign ruled by the Moon and focuses on themes like safety, feelings, home, and family. The Sun in Cancer can increase well-being through self-actualization by fostering environments where emotional security, privacy, and care are prioritized. Themes related to enhancing well-being through self-actualization could include nurturing oneself and others, building emotional intelligence, and creating a supportive environment. Below are some reflection questions that can be used to reflect upon values related to the process of self-actualization inspired by the Sun in Cancer.

- Do you value developing emotional intelligence by becoming more aware of your emotions and the emotions of others? If so, how do you incorporate this into your daily life?

- What do you consider comfortable or safe regarding your home environment?
- Do you see the connection between personal safety and growth? If so, how do you express and nurture that in your daily life?
- To what extent do you value building and maintaining strong relationships with family?
- Do you value engaging in roles that allow you to care for and support others, whether in your personal life or through volunteer or professional opportunities?

Sun in Leo

The Sun in Leo radiates warmth, creativity, and a strong sense of self. Leo is a fire sign ruled by the Sun and is associated with leadership, self-confidence, and a desire to be playful, recognized, and admired. Harnessing the qualities of the Sun in Leo to enhance well-being through self-actualization could involve cultivating self-expression, leadership, and personal integrity by embracing creativity and personal leadership. Below are some reflection questions that can be used to reflect upon values related to the process of self-actualization inspired by the Sun in Leo.

- How do you value practicing personal creativity through creative expression, such as painting, music, writing, or drama?
- Do you value playfulness? If so, how do you nurture your childlike nature?
- Do you take on leadership roles by leading initiatives that matter to you? If so, how, and when?
- How do you value the concept of self-expression, and what does that mean to you?
- How do you work with fostering a positive self-image and robust self-esteem?

Sun in Virgo

The Sun in Virgo highlights qualities of meticulousness, practicality, and a deep sense of duty. Virgo is an earth sign ruled by Mercury and is known for its analytical skills, attention to detail, and a focus on improvement and service. The Sun in Virgo can promote well-being through self-actualization through a detailed and service-oriented approach. By focusing on precision, practical problem-solving, health, service, and continual improvement, you can enhance personal development but also contribute effectively to the well-being of others, fulfilling the higher levels of Maslow's hierarchy of needs known as self-transcendence. Below are some reflection questions that can be used to reflect upon values related to the process of self-actualization inspired by the Sun in Virgo.

- Do you find it valuable to engage in activities or projects that require planning and attention to detail?
- Do you value having a daily routine that prioritizes your physical and mental health? If so, how?
- How do you relate to the concept of being of service and helping others, and how do you relate this process to the fostering of self-actualization and personal growth?
- How do you balance the need for perfection versus pragmatism regarding your identity?
- How do your personal values align with what you choose to do daily?

Sun in Libra

The Sun in Libra brings qualities of balance, harmony, and a strong inclination towards relationships. Libra, an air sign ruled by Venus, is known for its diplomatic nature, aesthetic sense, and drive for fairness and justice. Enhancing well-being through self-actualizing the Sun in Libra could include cultivating interpersonal harmony, aesthetic appreciation, and diplomacy.

Below are some reflection questions that can be used to reflect upon values related to the process of self-actualization inspired by the Sun in Libra.

- To what extent do you value developing and maintaining healthy relationships with others?
- How do you balance your need for diplomacy with self-actualization?
- Do you value expressing your identity through aesthetics, beauty, or art? If so, how and to what extent?
- Do you value participating in activities or causes promoting fairness and justice? If so, how, and how does that relate to your personal growth?
- How do you balance weighing options carefully with the need to self-actualize through active decision-making?

Sun in Scorpio

The Sun in Scorpio brings an intensity, depth, and focus on transformation. Scorpio is a water sign ruled by Pluto and is known for its passion, resourcefulness, and strong desire to delve into the mysteries of life. Self-actualization for the Sun in Scorpio could involve embracing depth, fostering resilience, and pursuing transformative growth. Below are some reflection questions that can be used to reflect upon values related to the process of self-actualization inspired by the Sun in Scorpio:

- To what extent do you value exploring and understanding your deeper motivations and desires? How do you express this depth and your innermost desires?
- How do you relate to personal challenges? Are you able to see them as transformative opportunities for growth and self-improvement?
- Do you value committing deeply to your passions and long-term goals? If so, how?

- How do you maintain your boundaries and integrity to focus on your personal growth?
- How important is intimacy and desire? How can you express that through self-actualization?

Sun in Sagittarius

The Sun in Sagittarius connects to optimism, freedom, and a thirst for knowledge and expansion. Sagittarius is a fire sign ruled by Jupiter and is known for its adventurous spirit, philosophical outlook, and desire to explore both the physical and intellectual realms. Enhancing well-being through self-actualization for the Sun in Sagittarius could involve expanding horizons through adventure, pursuing learning, and embracing openness to new experiences. Below are some reflection questions that can be used to reflect upon values related to the process of self-actualization inspired by the Sun in Sagittarius.

- To what extent do you value freedom, adventure, and broadening your understanding of life? How do you express this theme practically?
- How do you relate to the concept of "lifelong learning"? And how do you incorporate that phrase into your journey of self-actualization?
- Do you value optimism and personal growth? If so, how do you act on that?
- Do you engage in philosophical or spiritual pursuits that challenge and refine your beliefs and values?
- Do you practice what you preach in terms of acting in line with your values and philosophical beliefs?

Sun in Capricorn

The Sun in Capricorn embodies discipline, responsibility, and ambition. Capricorn is an earth sign ruled by Saturn and is known for its pragmatic approach to life, focus on achievements, and strong work ethic. Working with increasing well-being through self-actualization for the Sun in Capricorn could include setting and achieving realistic goals, fostering resilience, and maintaining integrity and discipline. Below are some reflection questions that can be used to reflect upon values related to the process of self-actualization inspired by the Sun in Capricorn.

- Do you establish clear, tangible goals that are aligned with your deepest values and ambitions? How do you act on these goals in your daily life?
- How do you relate to the word "resilience" in terms of your self-actualization process?
- Which responsibilities do you value and wish to maintain? Are there certain responsibilities you can let go of to make room for what really aligns with your personal expression?
- How do you manage the balance between work and personal development activities?
- Do you see value in the self-actualization process of both being a mentor and allowing yourself to be mentored by others? If so, how do you express that in your daily life?

Sun in Aquarius

The Sun in Aquarius embodies innovation, individuality, and a strong inclination towards humanitarianism. Aquarius, an air sign ruled by Uranus, is known for its forward-thinking approach, desire for social change, and preference for thinking outside the box. Enhancing well-being through self-actualization for the Sun in Aquarius could involve embracing uniqueness, fostering community connections, and advocating for progressive ideas. Below are some reflection questions that can be used to reflect upon values related to the process of self-actualization inspired by the Sun in Aquarius.

- Do you value pursuing interests and hobbies that allow you to express your unique self? If so, how?
- To what extent do you value and express being part of a community where you can contribute to collective efforts that bring about change?
- How does your self-actualization process include progressive changes and "thinking outside the box"?
- How do you relate to diversity, both in terms of your own self-expression and through connection to others?
- Do you value learning and exploring new ideas, technologies, or theories as part of your self-actualization journey? If so, how do you express that in daily life?

Sun in Pisces

The Sun in Pisces embodies empathy, deep emotional understanding, and a connection to the spiritual or transcendent aspects of life. Pisces, a Neptune-ruled water sign, is known for its sensitivity, artistic inclination, and intuitive nature. Enhancing well-being through self-actualization for the Sun in Pisces could involve embracing emotional depth, fostering creativity, and engaging in spiritual exploration that broadens the human experience. Below are some reflection questions that can be used to reflect upon values related to the process of self-actualization inspired by the Sun in Pisces.

- To what extent do you value empathy and compassion in your interactions? And how do you balance that with also caring for yourself?
- How do you value expressing yourself through music, poetry, painting, or other creative outlets? And how do you practically incorporate those expressions into your daily life?
- Do you value exploring spiritual practices or philosophies that resonate with your personal beliefs? If so, how do you

express these activities as part of your self-actualization journey?

- To what extent do you allow yourself to act and express yourself in alignment with your intuition?
- Do you value exploring yourself through the connection with universal consciousness? If so, how?

The Moon: Self-Compassion

Before we move on to the other planets, we must not forget that the Sun has an opposite in Earth's satellite – the Moon. If the Sun represents our conscious, active self, the Moon is our inner, more hidden, and *reactive self*. The Sun wants to shine, while the Moon wants to *receive* the Sun's light. The cycle of the Moon consists of 28 days and is represented by different lunar phases. The cyclical energy of the moon represents an ebb and flow, which is expressed in you via your emotions and the fluctuations felt in your inner world.

Other astrologers have defined the Moon's function in astrology. For example, astrologer April Elliott Kent describes the Moon as "your inner mom" and "the way you protect yourself, comfort yourself, and take care of others based on how you were cared for." Her key words for the Moon are "comfort," "nurturing," "security," "home," and "family." Astrologer Steven Forrest defines the Moon as "the development of the ability to feel or respond emotionally" and "the development of subjectivity, impressionability, and sensitivity" as well as "the development of what we might call a soul." He also presents some key questions related to the Moon, such as "What kinds of experiences are most essential to my happiness?" "When moodiness and irrationality overtake me, how are they expressed?" and "What unconscious emotional needs motivate my behavior?" According to me, the psychological concept of *self-compassion* aligns well with the astrological energy of the Moon, mainly through the emphasis on emotional nurturing, introspection, caring, and sensitivity. These elements resonate with the Moon's role in astrology as a symbol of feelings, emotional responses, and instinctual care. Let's explore these connections further by zooming in on the psychological concept known as self-compassion.

Self-compassion is a concept developed by Dr Kristin Neff, and involves treating oneself with the same kindness, concern, and support that one would show to a good friend. Key aspects of self-compassion include being gentle and understanding with oneself instead of harshly critical or judgmental, and recognizing that suffering and personal inadequacy are part of *the shared human experience* and not something that happens only to oneself. Lastly, the third component includes being mindful about one's emotions (without over-identifying with them), and through that allowing for a more nuanced approach to all feelings, including those we might experience as "negative." The psychological concept of self-compassion mirrors the archetypal energy of the Moon through its emphasis on emotional nurturing, introspection, and caring sensitivity. Both concepts advocate for a compassionate and understanding approach to dealing with personal emotions and challenges. Self-compassion enhances emotional well-being by promoting kindness towards oneself, recognizing the universality of human experiences, and maintaining a mindful balance of one's emotions, all of which resonate deeply with the nurturing and protective qualities associated with the Moon. Understanding these parallels can help individuals harness both psychological insights and astrological symbolism to foster a deeper connection with their inner selves and enhance their emotional resilience.

Working with self-compassion according to the Moon could be explored by treating oneself with understanding and gentleness during times of pain or failure. This, like the Moon, represents the "mothering" or nurturing that we apply to ourselves, much like a mother's compassion towards a child.

By recognizing that all feelings matter, and that suffering and imperfections are universal, we can potentially reduce isolation by acknowledging a shared human experience in regard to this theme. In astrology, the notion that we all have a moon in our chart can help emphasize the understanding that the ability to "mother" oneself is universal across genders, cultures, and other personal differences. Working with self-compassion and combining it with our understanding of the Moon can spark emotional healing by allowing us to comfort ourselves to a greater extent. We all need a mother, and we all have an emotional compass that can guide us towards greater emotional fulfillment and a sense of safety. Knowing what we now know, we can work with the Moon by asking ourselves:

> "How can I come in contact with a more nurturing and self-compassionate side of myself?"

Self-Compassion and Well-Being

Practicing self-compassion is closely linked to well-being as it can help foster emotional resilience, mental health, and overall life satisfaction. Practicing self-compassion can also help us to better cope with negative emotions by providing a supportive and understanding relationship to ourselves, promoting emotional stability.[18] In sum, research supports the connection between practicing self-compassion and experiencing greater well-being, as individuals with higher levels of self-compassion have been shown to report greater psychological well-being, lower levels of stress and anxiety, and increased life satisfaction[19].

---

[18] Neff, K. D. (2003). Self-compassion: An alternative conceptualization of a healthy attitude toward oneself. *Self and Identity*, 2(2), 85–101.

[19] Neff, K. D., & Germer, C. K. (2013). A pilot study and randomized controlled trial of the mindful self-compassion program. *Journal of Clinical Psychology*, *69*(1), 2844.

Enhance Well-Being through Self-Compassion: The Moon through the Signs

Moon in Aries

The Moon in Aries is ruled by Mars and could benefit from practicing self-compassion that includes nurturing one's energy and vitality, assertiveness, and pioneering spirit. This placement brings a focus on independence, courage, and inspiration, which can be harnessed to strengthen one's approach to self-compassion. Proactive self-care could include maintaining acceptance in regard to the fact that emotional expressions could be passionate and quick, and sometimes even be experienced as a bit impulsive or harsh. That is okay, as long as we see it and nurture ourselves as we would with a child. To increase self-compassion, you could potentially:

- Encourage yourself to assert your needs and personal boundaries as a form of self-kindness. Recognize that it's okay to prioritize your well-being and take decisive action to care for your emotional health.
- Practice mindfulness by acknowledging and validating your emotions without judgment. Allow yourself to feel and express anger, frustration, or any strong emotions, understanding them as natural and valid responses to your experiences.
- Use emotional challenges as opportunities for personal growth. Approach personal development with courage and the willingness to confront and learn from difficult emotional situations. This proactive stance can help transform negative self-criticisms into lessons for self-improvement.
- Practice forgiving yourself swiftly for mistakes (such as impulsivity or outbursts) and focus on moving forward with new lessons learned. This could help maintain

emotional momentum and prevent prolonged periods of self-criticism.

Moon in Taurus

The Moon in Taurus brings a calm, grounding influence on the practice of self-compassion, emphasizing stability, patience, and a strong connection to the physical senses. Taurus is known for its love of comfort, beauty, and a slow and steady approach to life. By combining these qualities with the principles of self-compassion, you can develop a nurturing and sustainable practice that enhances well-being and emotional stability. You could potentially:

- Nurture yourself by allowing yourself to seek pleasurable experiences such as decorating your personal spaces or decorating your home with items that please the senses, like soft textiles, pleasant aromas, or soothing colors. Allow yourself to create a physically comforting environment where you can completely rest.
- Mother yourself by focusing on activities that nurture your body, such as taking regular exercise, eating nourishing food, and having restful sleep. Allow yourself to prioritize physical health as a fundamental part of your self-care and apply self-compassion to avoid becoming too rigid around these practices. Balance is key.
- Encourage a mindset of patience with yourself and your emotional growth. Acknowledge that personal development takes time and that setbacks are part of the journey by practicing patience and self-kindness to reduce self-judgment.
- Allow yourself to spend time in natural settings and enjoy simple pleasures to ground yourself and connect with the Earth. Activities like gardening, hiking, or walking in a park can help center yourself and soothe

your emotions if you find yourself stuck in emotional processes.

Moon in Gemini

Working with self-compassion for the Mercury-ruled Moon in Gemini could include nurturing your needs for adaptability, communication, mental stimulation, and curiosity. Gemini is an air sign known for its versatility and desire for variety. Integrating this with the practice of self-compassion can foster an approach to emotions and nurturing that enhances the acceptance of emotional flexibility. To work with self-compassion for the Moon in Gemini, you could potentially:

- Allow yourself to express feelings and thoughts openly and flexibly through journaling, talking to friends, or therapeutic conversations. Communication can serve as a powerful tool for processing emotions and reducing feelings of isolation. But remember to reduce the burden of trying to "understand emotions" that we all tend to get caught in from time to time. Observe this from a point of common humanity and ease back to emotional curiosity.
- Use your intellectual curiosity to learn about and reflect upon emotions and psychological well-being and consider expressing your curiosity as a form of self-care. There is no need to make sense of it all or draw any conclusions, as the act of simply exploring can be an act of self-compassion in itself.
- Incorporate a variety of self-care activities into your routine to keep it engaging and fun. This could include trying different exercises, exploring new hobbies, or alternating between various meditation or relaxation techniques. Variety helps maintain interest and can make self-care more enjoyable and effective. It is okay to not stick to a rigid self-care routine!

- Explore the concept of common humanity through social interactions to process potential feelings of loneliness. Allow yourself to be nurtured through diverse insights on how others tend to cope with life's challenges, without pressuring yourself to do exactly like the others.

Moon in Cancer

The Moon in Cancer highlights emotional depth, nurturing, and sensitivity. Cancer is a water sign ruled by the Moon, so here the Moon is in its "home sign." The Moon in Cancer has a strong connection to emotions, comfort, and caring for oneself and others by creating safety and a sense of belonging. To increase self-compassion for the Moon in Cancer, you could potentially:

- Reflect upon how you can create a safe and nurturing space for yourself where you can be vulnerable and process your emotions without fear of judgment. This could involve exploring what it means to be surrounded by supportive and empathetic company and allowing yourself to set boundaries as a way to nurture yourself.
- Allow yourself to feel and express a full range of emotions with acceptance and without falling into judgment. Use mindfulness to observe and accept your emotions and recognize their potential fluctuation as natural and valid.
- Apply your natural nurturing abilities towards yourself by engaging in self-care practices that comfort and soothe you, such as cooking a nourishing meal, taking a warm bath, or other activities that somehow reinforce the importance of caring for your own needs too.
- Reflect upon your connections with your family or chosen family as a source of emotional support and comfort. Do you allow yourself to share feelings and experiences with loved ones that you feel safe around? Remember that it is

common for all humans to need support and to feel safe and emotionally grounded.

Moon in Leo

The Moon in Leo brings a vibrant, expressive, and heartfelt energy to the practice of self-compassion. Leo is a fire sign ruled by the Sun and is associated with warmth, generosity, creativity, and a strong sense of self. These characteristics can be beautifully integrated into self-compassion practices, emphasizing self-esteem, confidence, and the joyous expression of creativity and play, potentially by doing the following:

- Use your creative outlets such as drama, play, painting, writing, dancing, or any form of artistic expression to explore and express your feelings in a playful, expressive way. Creativity can be a powerful tool, and even the less "fun" feelings can be expressed through creativity or play.
- Allow yourself to show the same warmth and generosity to yourself that you would offer to others. Treat yourself with kindness, forgive yourself for mistakes, and support your own needs with enthusiasm and generosity.
- Engage in activities that bring you joy and allow you to connect with others in light-hearted, playful ways. But remember that even though social connections can enhance your mood and provide support, it is also important that you make time to care for yourself by nurturing your needs.
- Dare to see your own needs and stand up for yourself in situations where you might feel like your boundaries are challenged by remembering to talk to yourself as you would to a friend. Practice assertiveness as a form of self-compassion to help ensure that your needs are met and your self-esteem is nurtured.

Moon in Virgo

With the Moon in Virgo, the approach to self-compassion is influenced by Virgo's ruling planet, Mercury, and the characteristics of meticulousness, practicality, and a strong inclination towards improvement and service. Virgo is an earth sign that values order, usefulness, and attention to detail. Integrating these traits into the practice of self-compassion can lead to a structured, thoughtful, and nurturing approach that emphasizes wellness and self-improvement, potentially by doing the following:

- Incorporate daily practical self-care habits that support physical and mental health. This could include maintaining a balanced diet, establishing a regular sleep schedule, and organizing your living space to reduce stress and increase efficiency. Just be aware, so that these activities are expressed in a balanced and authentic way, beyond rigidity and perfectionism.
- Practice self-kindness by talking to yourself as your best friend. Set realistic and achievable goals for yourself and remind yourself of the concept of "good enough." Remember that all humans struggle with setbacks and harsh self-criticism. That's okay; just be sure to give yourself a pat on the shoulder from time to time.
- Channel any critical energy into constructive self-criticism to grow your sense of safety. Approach your limitations with kindness and a desire to grow, rather than judgment. Reframe critical thoughts into supportive feedback that motivates change and fosters resilience. Talk to your inner child as the healing mother you are.
- Engage in meaningful activities that help others in ways that also nurture your own emotions. This not only benefits those you help but also builds self-esteem and provides a sense of purpose and connection to yourself.

Moon in Libra

With the Moon in Libra, self-compassion can be practiced by embracing Libra's traits of balance and harmony, a strong orientation towards relationships, and aesthetic appreciation. Libra is an air sign ruled by Venus and connects to fairness, peace, and connectivity. These attributes can enhance the practice of self-compassion by focusing on emotional balance, interpersonal harmony, and the appreciation of beauty and comfort – possibly by doing the following:

- Focus on balancing several emotional needs by recognizing when you are pushing yourself too hard or neglecting your needs, and adjust accordingly to ensure a healthy balance in your daily activities. It is okay to seek harmony through others, but harmony can also be nurtured within yourself!
- Reflect upon how you define "supportive relationships" and how they contribute to your emotional well-being. Talk to yourself as you would talk to a friend, and engage in open communication that nurtures supportive networking to reinforce your sense of self-worth and emotional health.
- Incorporate elements of beauty and comfort into your environment, whether through art, music, or decor, to enhance your mood and overall sense of well-being. Appreciating beauty can be a form of self-care that uplifts the spirit and nurtures you on an emotional level.
- Allow yourself to be as fair to yourself as you are to others. Avoid self-criticism that is harsher than the criticism you would level at anyone else. Remember that we are all just humans by giving yourself the same understanding and forgiveness that you offer to friends and loved ones.

Moon in Scorpio

The astrological placement of the Moon in Scorpio adds a unique depth and intensity to the practice of self-compassion due to its ruling planet Pluto. The Moon in Scorpio is known for its deep emotional currents, powerful insights, and transformative energies, making the practice of self-compassion both profound and potentially healing. Integrating the psychological definition of self-compassion with the characteristics of the Moon in Scorpio can enhance emotional resilience and personal growth, potentially through doing the following:

- Practice self-kindness and acknowledge and accept your deep emotions without judgment. Emotional intensity does not have to be shameful and can be channeled into a powerful self-awareness that accepts all parts of oneself, including those that are painful or difficult to face.
- Use mindfulness to observe your feelings from a more neutral point of view and recognize that just because it feels like pain, it can still offer opportunities for growth and transformation. Allow yourself to gently transform negative self-criticisms into self-acceptance by talking to yourself as you would talk to a friend.
- Recognize that suffering and personal challenges are part of the human experience through the concept of common humanity. Acknowledge that everyone faces inner battles and approach this theme by incorporating your interest in investigation and depth, potentially via the study of psychology.
- Allow yourself to nurture supportive relationships that provide you with a sense of being deeply connected. Allow yourself to be vulnerable with a few trusted others to practice self-kindness and reduce emotional isolation. It is okay not to tell the whole world about your feelings,

but it can benefit you to be fully open with a few selected people you trust.

- Honor your need for privacy and set boundaries as a form of self-care. Learn to say no or step back when needed to take care of your emotional health, recognizing that solitude can also be a space for healing and self-reflection. It is okay to care for oneself this way and to need time to process emotional impressions in solitude.

Moon in Sagittarius

The Moon in Sagittarius infuses the emotional life with optimism, adventure, and a quest for meaning and truth. Sagittarius, a fire sign ruled by Jupiter, is known for its love of freedom and exploration and can be integrated with practicing self-compassion to foster emotional growth and maintain an optimistic perspective. Below are some practical ideas for how to practice self-compassion for the Moon in Sagittarius:

- Practice seeing emotionally charged challenges as opportunities for growth and learning. There is a lesson in every experience without needing to turn to "toxic positivity." Practice the art of "active hope" by acknowledging your feelings from a growth perspective in order to align your actions with your feelings and nurture your needs.
- Create space in your life for emotional freedom. We all have our individual preferences, so allow yourself to come in contact with what makes you feel emotionally nurtured and free. This may mean setting boundaries in relationships, managing your time for personal pursuits, or ensuring that your lifestyle allows for spontaneity as a means to care for yourself.
- Avoid running away from emotions. Instead, try approaching yourself like you would approach a friend

by incorporating humor into your daily life. Laughing with oneself and viewing life's absurdities from a higher perspective can be a powerful tool for maintaining emotional balance.

- Seek meaning as a way to practice self-care. Connect with subjects such as philosophy or other forms of explorative subjects. Nurture yourself through the knowledge that comes from expanding your horizons and accept the fact that constant expansion and creation of meaning is, in fact, a form of self-care for you.

Moon in Capricorn

The Moon in Capricorn brings a disciplined, responsible, and practical approach to the practice of self-compassion. Capricorn is an earth sign ruled by Saturn and values structure, ambition, and achievement. These characteristics can shape a self-compassion practice emphasizing resilience, and a pragmatic approach to emotions and emotional growth. Below is some practical advice for how to practice self-compassion for the Moon in Capricorn:

- Develop strategies to cope with less pleasurable feelings related to setbacks and challenges. Viewing difficult experiences as opportunities for growth and learning can help maintain a balanced emotional life, self-compassion, motivation, and commitment.
- Implement routines and structures that support your well-being, whether they are related to your physical surroundings or your emotions. This might include regular exercise, a healthy diet, and sufficient sleep. A structured approach to daily life can increase self-care and is ultimately a form of self-compassion.
- Dare to seek advice and mentorship from others instead of falling into the trap of needing to solve everything

by yourself. Allow others to provide perspectives to your emotional experiences and remember that we all struggle sometimes. By practicing mindfulness and non-judgment, you can reach out and dare to open up and reduce feelings of isolation.

- Recognize that rest and downtime are just as important as acting on your ambitions in order to maintain health and prevent feeling exhausted. Integrate periods of rest into your structured routine and treat these moments as necessary for long-term success and well-being, not as a deviation from your goals. Apply compassion and remember that all humans need to rest.

Moon in Aquarius

The Moon in Aquarius brings a unique, innovative, and humanitarian approach to the emotional life and the practice of self-compassion. Aquarius is an air sign ruled by Uranus and is associated with individuality, intellectual independence, and a focus on social progress. Below are some suggestions that can help foster a self-compassion practice suitable for the Moon in Aquarius:

- Encourage yourself to honor your individuality and uniqueness as a self-care practice. Practice accepting and loving yourself as you are by talking to yourself as your own best friend. Reflect upon what makes you unique. Acknowledge and nurture that without conforming to societal expectations. Recognize and celebrate your quirks and personal traits as strengths, not flaws.
- Connect with others but remember to also cultivate a healthy level of emotional freedom for yourself. Practice self-compassion by ensuring that you are totally accepted and loved, even if you are not overly dependent on external validation or relationships.

- Experiment with unconventional methods of self-care despite what others might think. Dare to nurture your inventive nature through creative and unusual practices and remember that what unites us humans is that we are all unique in our own sense!
- Foster a sense of safety by engaging with communities and groups that reflect your innermost values and as a way to nurture yourself. Connect with others who share similar passions and increase your sense of belonging by daring to be led by your unique interests.

Moon in Pisces

The Moon in Pisces brings a deeply empathetic, sensitive, intuitive, and compassionate energy to the emotional life. Pisces, a water sign ruled by Neptune, is known for its sensitivity, imagination, and a strong connection to emotions and spirituality. Below are some ideas of self-compassion practices that are potentially valuable for the Moon in Pisces:

- Nurture your sensitivity and learn to see it as a superpower. Tend to your feelings and learn to discern your feelings from those of others. Treat your emotions with kindness and understanding by applying the same empathy towards yourself as you do towards others.
- Use arts and creativity as a therapeutic tool for mindfully expressing your emotions and experiences. Activities like painting, writing, music, or dance can be powerful ways to process and express feelings, contributing to emotional care and self-compassion.
- Explore spiritual practices that resonate with you, whether it's meditation, prayer, nature walks, or yoga. Spirituality can offer comfort, provide a sense of belonging, and help you feel grounded, which enhances self-compassion.

- Regularly set aside time to be alone with yourself in a peaceful setting, preferably by the sea. Let go of any potential guilt and approach yourself as your best friend by listening to your own advice by connecting with your inner self and recharging your emotional batteries in solitude.

Mercury: Curiosity

Now that we have explored our two luminaries, the Sun and the Moon, it is time to move on to the next planet from the Sun: Mercury! Mercury is a small, fast-moving planet that many astrologers refer to as "the messenger." To exemplify Mercury's role, we can imagine that the identity (the Sun) wants to communicate its energy and does so via its messenger (Mercury).

Let us begin by taking a look at how other astrologers have defined Mercury's energy. Astrologer April Elliott Kent describes Mercury as "your inner sidekick" and representative of perception, communication, and skill, while Steven Forrest defines Mercury's function as "intelligence," "transmission of information; talking, teaching, writing," and "reception of information; listening, learning, reading, observing." He continues by stating a few key questions related to Mercury, such as "What are my intellectual and communicative strengths?" and "What are my intellectual and communicative weaknesses?" It is clear that Mercury rules communication, intellect, and the exchange of information, and while I agree with Steven's definition that includes both *active components*, such as talking, teaching, and writing, and *passive and receptive components*, such as listening, learning, reading, and observing, I want to develop his perspective by moving beyond the concept of *strengths and weaknesses*. Instead, I want to remind you that this book aims to broaden our understanding of astrology by connecting it to values and a valued life direction. From this perspective, we can hypothesize that Mercury could be mirrored by *curiosity,* which would then include *both* active and passive/receptive components of communication and perception while emphasizing that curiosity, in itself, could be seen as a character strength that could be explored by how we choose to express it in our everyday life.

Curiosity, as identified in psychological researchers Martin Seligman and Christopher Peterson's[20] book of character strengths within positive psychology, refers to an individual's interest in ongoing experience for its own sake through the exploration and discovery of new things, involving a desire to learn more about *anything* and *everything*. Curiosity is associated with an openness to experience, where one continually seeks to understand how things work and to engage with the world inquisitively. This character strength enables individuals to embrace novel situations, challenges, and learning opportunities, often leading to greater personal growth and fulfillment. Curiosity motivates people to venture beyond their comfort zones, leading to richer experiences and broader knowledge. This concept can also be understood as "the recognition, pursuit, and intense desire to explore novel, challenging, and uncertain events."[21]

I think curiosity aligns well with the astrological interpretation of Mercury, as both curiosity and Mercury emphasize the pursuit of understanding and the mechanisms of exchanging and discovering new information. The interesting part is that curiosity is hypothesized to be important in both *active* and *receptive communication,* which mirrors Steven Forrest's (1988) definition of Mercury. Overall, curiosity

---

[20] Peterson, C., & Seligman, M. E. (2004). *Character Strengths and Virtues: A handbook and classification* (Vol. 1). New York: Oxford University Press.

[21] Kashdan, T. B., & Silvia, P. J. (2011). Curiosity and interest: The benefits of thriving on novelty and challenge. In S. J. Lopez & C. R. Snyder (eds), *The Oxford Handbook of Positive Psychology* (2nd edn, pp. 367–75). New York: Oxford University Press.

highlights adaptability as individuals learn from new situations and integrate knowledge, which mirrors Mercury's fast energy. Based on what we now know, we can redefine our understanding of Mercury by connecting it to curiosity, and connect it to the reflection question below:

"How do I express and explore my curiosity?"

Curiosity and Well-Being

Curiosity connects to the science of well-being because it is thought to drive personal growth, engagement, and life satisfaction. It contributes to well-being in several ways, leading to greater engagement in activities and learning. When people are curious, they are more likely to immerse themselves in new experiences, which can favor "flow states" (see Mars for the connection to engagement) and increased enjoyment, as individuals with high levels of curiosity report greater life satisfaction, better psychological well-being, and more frequent experiences of positive emotions.[22]

Enhance Well-Being through Curiosity: Mercury through the Signs

Mercury in Aries

The astrological placement of Mercury in Aries is ruled by Mars and brings a dynamic and assertive style to communication and thinking, characterized by directness, enthusiasm, and a pioneering approach. Working with Mercury in Aries to increase well-being through curiosity could potentially be done in the following ways:

[22] Kashdan, T. B., & Steger, M. F. (2007). Curiosity and pathways to well-being and meaning in life: Traits, states, and everyday behaviors. *Motivation and Emotion, 31,* 159–73.

- Channel your curious energy into starting new projects that really spark your interest. Whether it is learning a new skill, starting a hobby, or exploring new intellectual pursuits, the act of initiating new activities can stimulate your mind and keep you engaged, enhancing your overall happiness and satisfaction. Do not fall into the trap of comparing yourself to others. If anything, your character strength is your ability to come up with ideas and projects through your passionate curiosity!
- Find comfort and self-acceptance in the practice of daring to make decisions quickly and confidently based on identifying what makes you passionate and curious. Trust that your curiosity leads you on to the right path!

Mercury in Taurus

Mercury in Taurus, ruled by Venus, adds a practical element to communication and curiosity and can be favored by allowing oneself to spend time in deep contemplation about subjects and delve into topics at a slow and steady pace. This placement values thorough understanding over skimming the surface. Working with Mercury in Taurus to increase well-being through curiosity could potentially be done in the following ways:

- Nurture your curiosity in a hands-on, steady, and meaningful way. Explore and be curious about the tangible aspects of the world by channeling your curiosity into pursuits that also involve your senses.
- Apply compassion and acceptance to the fact that embracing learning often requires time and patience and that enjoyment can be felt during the process as well. Directing your curiosity towards long-term activities such as gradually mastering a skill or contributing to a project as it develops over time can potentially help boost your psychological well-being by acting on your curiosity.

Mercury in Gemini

Mercury in Gemini thrives on variety and mental stimulation and often enjoys learning a little bit about everything and engaging in a wide range of learning activities. Working with Mercury in Gemini to increase well-being through curiosity could potentially be done in the following ways:

- Practice playful learning and explore joyful ways to satisfy your curiosity, which can lead to innovative discoveries and personal growth. Keep in mind that whatever you are curious about can be explored as a means, not an end. Have fun and enjoy your curious endeavors by being in the moment!
- Embrace, accept, and express your curiosity through various intellectual and social activities, and potentially enhance your overall well-being by keeping yourself mentally active and socially connected.

Mercury in Cancer

Mercury in Cancer blends curiosity and intellectual stimulation with emotional and intuitive qualities to foster social connections through nurturing communication. Exploring well-being via the curiosity that Mercury in Cancer expresses could be done in the following ways:

- Engage in activities that connect you with your roots or heritage, such as exploring family memoirs or your heritage. Directing curiosity towards these subjects could provide a deeper sense of identity and belonging and might help increase your overall well-being.
- Apply curiosity towards allowing your intuition to guide you further. Develop trust in your "gut feeling" and see how that can help you feel more content in life.

Mercury in Leo

When Mercury is in Leo, curiosity is often channeled in an expressive and confident way. This placement enjoys being noticed and appreciated, thriving on the sharing and exchange of ideas in a vibrant, creative manner. Below are some ideas for how to work with the energy of Mercury in Leo, and use curiosity to spark well-being:

- Dedicate time to expressing your curiosity towards subjects that captivate you, preferably something creative that sparks your passion. Passion-driven learning could enhance well-being by aligning your activities with your true interests.
- Remember to incorporate elements of fun and play into your learning processes or curious endeavors. By letting your curiosity lead you to passion, others can get inspired to do the same!

Mercury in Virgo

Mercury in Virgo tends to express a focus on details through analytical strengths. Mercury in Virgo excels in precision, practicality, and efficiency and could be expressed via the following suggestions:

- Allow for practical applications of any knowledge gained, and use your curiosity to solve real-world problems through tangible solutions. Channeling your curiosity into projects or activities that result in something tangible, like helping others, could give a sense of reward or fulfillment, which ultimately could help increase well-being.
- Allow yourself to let your curiosity lead you towards mastering a skill or an area of knowledge. Striving for

mastery can be deeply fulfilling, although it is important to explore it through the lens of passion and pragmatism, rather than perfectionism.

Mercury in Libra

Mercury in Libra tends to express curiosity in a diplomatic, balanced, and social manner through its emphasis on harmony, social relations, and aesthetic appreciation. Below are some examples of how to use your curiosity to create well-being according to Mercury in Libra:

- Let your curiosity guide you to participate in activities that focus on exploring different viewpoints rather than winning arguments. This kind of intellectual engagement promotes a greater understanding of complex issues and might help you make use of your curiosity in a constructive way.
- Identify what makes you intellectually stimulated and curious by exploring subjects and activities oriented towards understanding others, exploring artistic and cultural fields, and subjects covering themes of balance and fairness.

Mercury in Scorpio

Mercury in Scorpio is ruled by Pluto and tends to bring a deep, investigative, and often intense approach to curiosity, communication, and thinking. Below are some ideas for how to channel the curiosity of Mercury in Scorpio to enhance well-being:

- Allow yourself to explore your curiosity regarding uncovering secrets, exploring hidden truths, and delving into the mysteries of the human psyche. Just be mindful if you fall into obsession, and then lovingly observe and

let go. Uncovering truths or exploring depths should be fun and rewarding, not keep you in a grip.
- Turn your curiosity inwards through practices or self-reflection activities like journaling or meditation that encourage introspection. Understanding your inner depths can lead to greater self-awareness and well-being.

Mercury in Sagittarius

Mercury in Sagittarius is ruled by Jupiter and gives curiosity expressed through this sign a flavor of exploration, big ideas, and a quest for meaning. Below are some ideas for how to express this energy in a way that could help increase well-being:

- Allow your curiosity to guide you towards exploring and engaging with the world in an open and enthusiastic way, either through physical travel or through books and other resources. Embody a broad and expansive approach to life to enhance your well-being.
- Actively seek out information and viewpoints and keep curiously challenging your beliefs. Engaging with diverse perspectives broadens your understanding and could strengthen your critical thinking and adaptability.

Mercury in Capricorn

Mercury in Capricorn brings a structured, disciplined, and pragmatic approach to communication and thought processes through its ruling planet, Saturn. Reflect upon the examples below to come in contact with whatever might help you express your curiosity and make you thrive:

- Reflect upon how you can direct your curiosity towards subjects that allow you to apply knowledge in a useful and concrete way. By expressing curiosity towards systematic learning, focused research, and practical problem-solving, your well-being could perhaps receive a boost.

- Explore your curiosity about subjects covering the past to help you understand how past events and cultures have shaped and impacted our current society. A deeper understanding of the world could indeed help spark your curiosity and enhance your sense of belonging.

Mercury in Aquarius

Mercury in Aquarius is ruled by Uranus and therefore brings a unique, innovative, and often unconventional approach to thinking and communication. Below are some ideas for how to work with directing one's curiosity, as described by Mercury in Aquarius:

- Explore how you can enhance your sense of well-being by directing your curiosity towards subjects that are progressive and forward-thinking, such as questioning conventional ideas, and by being open to new ideas and focused on solving complex societal issues.
- Allow yourself to seek out alternative educational models, such as online courses, or self-directed learning projects that allow you to explore subjects at your own pace and in your own style. This flexibility can make learning more enjoyable and help spark your sense of well-being.

Mercury in Pisces

Mercury in Pisces brings a dreamy, intuitive, and often empathetic quality to thinking and communication due to its planetary ruler, Neptune. This placement is known for its deep emotional intelligence, imaginative thought processes, and a tendency to blur the lines between reality and fantasy. Below are some ideas for how to work with this placement to enhance well-being:

- Direct your curiosity to areas and subjects where imagination and creativity are preferred. This could be anything creative, such as music, poetry, painting, or photography. Embracing that curiosity beyond logical subjects could potentially help spark more well-being through acceptance of the fact that you are, in fact, more formless in your perception than most.
- Use your curiosity to practice and trust your intuition. Activities involving meditation, reflective journaling, intuition, or spirituality could help you tune into your intuitive senses and feel more aligned with yourself.

Venus: Harmony

After Mercury comes Venus, which orbits around the Sun in about 225 days. Venus symbolizes concepts such as love, desire, relationships, what we need and want, pleasure, beauty, wealth, money, and harmony. Venus is the second planet from the Sun and can be further understood by thinking about how the identity (Sun) expresses itself in communication via the messenger (Mercury), which then creates conditions for us to relate to others, express our needs, seek pleasure, and create harmony (Venus).

Before delving into how we can connect the astrological energy of Venus to modern psychological concepts of well-being, let us first take a look at how other astrologers have defined Venus. April Elliott Kent describes Venus as "your inner consort" and "what makes you feel good." She presents Venus as representative of money, relationships, beauty, and pleasure. Based on this, we can understand Venus in relation to concepts such as desires, values, finances, and partners. Steven Forrest defines Venus's function as "the restoration of equilibrium to the shattered sensitivity," "the stabilization of a network of supportive emotional bonds," and "the development of the capacity to make an aesthetic response." He continues by presenting Venus's key questions: "How can I calm down?" "What do I need in a partner?" "What can I bring to a relationship?" From my point of view, I think the astrological energy of Venus can be connected to the psychological concept of *harmony*. In psychology, harmony refers to a state of balance and agreement in feelings, actions, or relationships, promoting a peaceful and cooperative environment. Key aspects of harmony include striving for equilibrium in various aspects of life, such as work-life balance, emotional balance, and interpersonal balance. It involves striving for balance in various life areas by promoting stability and contentment through balance and flexibility in harmonizing different aspects within the world, which could be further explained by the quote: "Harmony is by its very nature relational. It is through mutual support and mutual dependence that things flourish."[23]

I believe that the psychological concept of harmony closely mirrors the archetypal energy of Venus in its emphasis on balance, relationships, aesthetic appreciation, and the pursuit of peace and cooperation. The psychological concept of harmony involves a sense of balance, peace, and congruence in one's life and relationships. It encompasses internal harmony, which relates to self-acceptance and coherence between one's values and actions, and external harmony, which involves positive and cooperative relationships with others and the environment. Both concepts highlight the importance of maintaining equilibrium in personal and interpersonal dynamics, appreciating beauty, and fostering peaceful and supportive interactions. Understanding these parallels helps illuminate the connections

---

[23] Li, C. (2008a). The ideal of harmony in ancient Chinese and Greek philosophy. *Dao*, 7(1), 81–98.

Li, C. (2008b). The philosophy of harmony in classical Confucianism. *Philosophy Compass*, 3(3), 13.

between psychological concepts and astrological symbolism, and highlights the transformative potential in seeking balance and harmony in our lives and relationships. Based on what we now know, we can go on and rephrase Steven's key question related to Venus so that it includes harmony, perhaps by asking the following:

> "How do I act in line with my values to foster more harmony in my life?"

Harmony and Well-Being

Harmony is closely connected to the science of well-being or positive psychology because it is thought to promote mental and emotional health, life satisfaction, and overall happiness, underscoring the importance of balance and positive relationships in achieving a fulfilling and happy life. It aligns with the broader goals of positive psychology by emphasizing the holistic nature of well-being, which includes internal and external aspects of a person's life. Recent studies indicate that individuals who strive for harmony in their lives and relationships experience lower stress levels and higher overall well-being.[24]

Enhance Well-Being through Harmony: Venus through the Signs

Venus in Aries

Venus in Aries brings a dynamic, enthusiastic, and assertive approach to relationships, aesthetics, and values, which

[24] Kjell, O. N. E., Daukantaitė, D., Hefferon, K., & Sikström, S. (2016). The harmony in life scale complements the satisfaction with life scale: Expanding the conceptualization of the cognitive component of subjective well-being. *Social Indicators Research, 126,* 893–919.

contrasts with Venus's typically harmonious and gentle nature. This placement encourages boldness and initiative in seeking pleasure and relationships. Integrating the psychological concept of harmony with Venus in Aries can potentially be done through the following suggestions:

- Foster harmonious relationships by daring to practice assertive communication techniques that allow you to express your needs and desires clearly and respectfully.
- Dare to step out of your comfort zone to initiate new social connections or romantic endeavors. Accept the fact that you might want to engage in new activities that can bring harmony to your life.
- Remind yourself to stop yourself mindfully and compassionately before acting on every impulse, especially in relationships or financial decisions. Dare to take a moment to reflect on the potential impacts of your actions on maintaining emotional equilibrium and ensure that your decisions contribute to an overall sense of harmony by aligning with your long-term well-being and goals.

Venus in Taurus

The astrological placement of Venus in Taurus emphasizes stability, sensuality, and a strong appreciation for the finer things in life. Venus in Taurus can be explored by seeking harmony in ways that resonate deeply with Taurus's earthy and pleasure-seeking traits, such as the following:

- Reflect upon the idea of having a budget that allows for both saving and the occasional indulgence in quality items that bring you joy. Financial stability can contribute to a sense of pleasure, but it should ideally be balanced with saving as well as treating oneself whenever possible.

- Enhance harmony by developing a consistent routine that includes relaxation and self-care, and by building and maintaining relationships that are supportive and genuine and that you truly enjoy.

Venus in Gemini

When Venus, the planet of love, beauty, and values, is in Gemini, the sign of communication, intellect, and social connections, it highlights the need to integrate flexibility in regard to harmony, potentially by doing the following:

- Increase your sense of harmony and well-being by actively engaging in social activities that stimulate intellectual discussion and playful interaction. Building a diverse social network can help create a balanced and harmonious social life.
- Work on improving your interpersonal communication by practicing active listening, clear articulation of your ideas, and openness to others' perspectives, and explore communication as a fundamental part of maintaining harmony in all relationships.

Venus in Cancer

Venus in Cancer approaches harmonious relationships with deep sensitivity, nurturing, and a strong desire for emotional security. Cancer's influence on Venus fosters an environment where emotional depth and familial connections are highlighted. People born with this placement can explore harmony in several ways, such as by doing the following:

- Value harmony in your relationships by being openly affectionate and supportive, ensuring that your relationships are reciprocal, with care and support flowing in both directions.

- Spend quality time with family members or those you consider family. Prioritize harmonious self-care by setting boundaries that protect your emotional well-being.

Venus in Leo

Venus in Leo brings a vibrant, expressive, and generous energy to relationships and personal values and promotes warmth, playfulness, and charisma. Exploring the concept of harmony through Venus in Leo could be done in the following ways:

- Value relationships that are based on mutual respect, joy, play, and the free exchange of affection. Celebrate and appreciate the strengths of others, and encourage a joyful, reciprocal exchange of energy in your interpersonal connections.
- Value yourself and strive for recognition without depending too much on external validation. Celebrate your own achievements and foster a sense of internal fulfillment and harmonious connection to yourself.

Venus in Virgo

Venus in Virgo has a sense of practicality, attention to detail, and a service-oriented approach to harmony. Below are some examples of how to work with Venus in Virgo to spark harmony and potentially enhance well-being:

- Enhance harmony through nurturing relationships where support and practical help are reciprocated. Acts of service such as helping a friend move, preparing meals for a loved one, or assisting in organizing someone's workspace can strengthen bonds and promote emotional balance. Just remember that you also deserve to receive help and that doing things for others is an act of kindness and not a must.

- Value yourself by incorporating a daily routine that includes regular exercise, a nutritious diet, and sufficient rest. Support your own harmony by taking care of your health!

Venus in Libra

Venus naturally rules Libra, making this placement particularly harmonious. Venus in Libra is often drawn to exploring interpersonal relationships, aesthetics and beauty, and a balanced approach to life. Integrating the qualities of Venus in Libra with the psychological concept of harmony could be done in the following ways:

- Develop relationships where both parties feel equally valued and respected, have shared responsibilities, and strive for compromises. Balanced relationships are foundational to mirroring one's own worth and could help contribute to a sense of overall well-being.
- Explore your relationship to art, beauty, or aesthetic expressions. Engaging with the arts can provide a sense of harmony, inspiration, and a deeper connection to your own sense of values.

Venus in Scorpio

Venus in Scorpio brings depth, intensity, and passion to relationships and is often characterized by strong desires, deep emotional connections, and a focus on transformation and authenticity. Below are some ideas for how to explore harmony for Venus in Scorpio:

- Foster deep relationships where vulnerability is embraced, and emotional depths are explored. Trust and emotional intimacy can significantly enhance relational harmony and personal well-being. Dare to be honest with yourself about what you really value in relationships to others.

- Reflect upon your values related to intimacy and sexuality. Healthy expression and acceptance of sexual or intimate desires could potentially enhance personal harmony and strengthen romantic partnerships.

Venus in Sagittarius

Venus in Sagittarius explores relationships, personal values, and the pursuit of beauty with a sense of adventure, freedom, and exploration. This placement emphasizes growth, optimism, and a desire for knowledge. Below are some ideas for how to work with this placement to increase well-being through harmony:

- Ask yourself to what extent you value an open-minded approach in your relationships and personal interests. Identify *your* truth and acknowledge how flexibility can help you bring more harmony into your life via personal relationships.
- Reflect upon whether positive thinking and optimism are part of your core values and how you express that in everyday life. Your mindset can help you navigate life's challenges while maintaining a sense of personal worth.

Venus in Capricorn

Venus in Capricorn brings a pragmatic, disciplined, and responsible approach to relationships, aesthetics, and values. This placement emphasizes stability, maturity, and long-term planning. Working with Venus in Capricorn to explore harmony could potentially be done in the following ways:

- Think about whether you prefer relationships that are based on trust, reliability, and a clear understanding of mutual expectations, and if so, be clear about your expectations and values. Stable, predictable relationships can favor harmony and a sense of security and well-being.

- Invite more overall harmony by reflecting upon your self-worth and ask yourself how you value yourself beyond accomplishments and achievements. Embrace the fact that although you might like to manage responsibilities, your self-worth lies beyond that.

Venus in Aquarius

Venus in Aquarius brings a unique, unconventional, and community-focused energy to relationships, aesthetics, and values. This placement emphasizes independence, innovation, and a strong sense of social justice, often prioritizing friendships and group affiliations over traditional relational norms. This is how you can work with Venus in Aquarius to foster harmony and a greater sense of well-being:

- Tap into your desire to express yourself in a way that reflects your true self, even if it diverges from societal norms. Seeing your worth and daring to cultivate a strong sense of individuality can enhance harmony and create a greater sense of well-being by aligning your external life with your internal values.
- Ask yourself how you can act in accordance with your values to create a harmonious life that not only satisfies your personal aspirations but also contributes positively to the broader community.

Venus in Pisces

Venus in Pisces brings a compassionate, empathetic, and deeply intuitive energy to relationships, beauty, and values. This placement emphasizes emotional depth, a strong sense of unity with others, and an affinity for transcendent or spiritual experiences. Harmony according to Venus in Pisces could be explored in the following ways:

- Reflect upon your values in regard to relationships and ask yourself if your current interpersonal relationships allow for emotional depth and vulnerability to the extent that you wish. Seek relationships where empathy is prioritized and cherished and reciprocal.
- Explore your own sense of self-worth by cherishing how you have been blessed with the capacity to express love, affection, and romance in a universal and almost otherworldly way. Empathy is a superpower, although our society tends to forget that it is.

Mars: Engagement

When we get past Venus, we meet Mars. In astrology, Mars represents passion, drive, initiation, sexuality, aggression, competitive instinct, and work. This symbolism is reflected astronomically as we see how Mars, unlike Mercury and Venus, can travel further away in its orbit around the Sun. Through Mars' ability to move further away from the Sun, we can see its willpower, action, and courage expressed. It takes about 22 months for Mars to make one circle around the Sun, which means that Mars spends an average of about six weeks in each zodiac sign. Steven Forrest describes Mars' function as "the development of will," "the expansion of courage," and "assertiveness training," with the key questions "What battles must I face?" "Where must I be more assertive if I am not to suffer pointless conflict and strife?" "How can I sharpen my will?" and "How do I express my aggressiveness?" April Elliott Kent defines Mars as an energy with astrological trademarks linked to our survival instinct comprised of initiative, action, anger, aggression, violence, competition, sexuality, and our urge to live.

As with all astrological energies, it is important to note that there is a wide range of expressions tied to an archetypal energy, which can impact the way it is expressed in our everyday lives. In the case of Mars, the term "action" can function as an example. To take action can mean so many things, as it can be symbolized by how well we manage to defend ourselves when we find ourselves encountering situations where our primal urge to live might be threatened. However, it can also mean how well we manage to take the initiative and act upon our wants and needs. On a similar note, there is a fine line between different expressions of Mars-ruled themes, such as assertiveness versus aggressiveness. A middle way is perhaps the concept of *agency*, which mirrors Mars by representing *action* and initiative, encouraging individuals to direct their focus towards their objectives by acting according to their values. This connects to the psychological concept of *engagement*, which is part of Martin Seligman's PERMA-model and is described as "being one with the music."[7] This way of understanding engagement is somewhat equivalent to the term "flow" and is described as complete absorption in activities and living in the present moment while focusing entirely on the task at hand.[25] As I read this, I found it logical to connect Mars with the phrase "complete absorption in activities and living in the present moment while focusing entirely on the task at hand," mainly since it reflects an act of energy and passion, both of which are central parts of the basic understanding for Mars. Furthermore, the state known as flow (engagement) requires that challenges should be in optimal balance with our skills and identified strengths.[26] From my perspective, this statement could further be linked to

[25] Csikszentmihalyi, M. (1990). *Flow: The psychology of optimal experience.* New York: Harper and Row.

[26] Csikszentmihalyi, M., & LeFevre, J. (1989). Optimal experience in work and leisure. *Journal of Personality and Social Psychology, 56*(5), 815–22.

Steven Forrest's question "What battles must I face?" and Mars' function as "the development of will," as well as April Elliott Kent's definition of Mars as equivalent to our urge to live. Both engagement and agency mirror the archetypal energy of Mars in their emphasis on action, motivation, and the drive to pursue goals with focus, determination, and confidence. Both concepts highlight the importance of being actively involved in activities.

Based on this, we understand that *engagement* and the related term *flow* both require an element of *challenge*. We also know that the challenges should be adjusted to match our skills. Thanks to research, we know that pursuing engagement and meaning are important when we strive to achieve well-being, and in fact, also seem to be more important indicators of well-being than pleasure.[27] Let us now go on and redefine Mars' reflection question:

> "What challenges do I want to commit to in order to increase my agency and feel more engaged and content with my life?"

Engagement and Well-Being

Engagement (similar to flow) is integral to achieving a fulfilling and meaningful life, as it involves deep involvement and optimal experiences that enhance one's quality of life. Research supports the connection between engagement/flow and well-being, as individuals who frequently experience flow tend to report higher levels of happiness and life satisfaction.[25] Similarly, engagement in meaningful activities has been linked to greater well-being and life satisfaction.[7]

---

[27] Schueller, S. M., & Seligman, M. E. (2010). Pursuit of pleasure, engagement, and meaning: Relationships to subjective and objective measures of well-being. *Journal of Positive Psychology*, *5*(4), 253–63.

Enhance Well-Being through Engagement: Mars through the Signs

Mars in Aries

Mars in Aries embodies assertiveness, directness, and a pioneering spirit, aligning well with the psychological concepts of "agency" and "engagement." Mars in Aries can enhance well-being by fostering assertiveness, initiative, and proactive engagement in various aspects of life, possibly by doing the following:

- Engage regularly in physical activities that challenge you, such as competitive sports or intensive exercise regimes, which can help increase your vitality while contributing to psychological engagement by keeping you energized and focused on the task at hand.
- Develop your sense of agency by asserting yourself and approaching personal and professional challenges with a proactive mindset. Tackling challenges head-on can boost your confidence, enhance your skills, and spark your engagement. However, make sure you have established your values so that you can act in accordance with them and avoid unnecessary impulsivity.

Mars in Taurus

Mars in Taurus channels Mars' assertive and dynamic energy into a more deliberate, persistent, and practical form. This astrological placement emphasizes steadiness, determination, and the pursuit of security, often focusing on long-term goals. Sparking engagement and increased agency for Mars in Taurus could be done in the following ways:

- Value and nurture your sense of agency by weighing the long-term benefits and consequences of your actions and persisting in challenges and acknowledging your ability to stick with difficult tasks or long-term goals without losing your focus or motivation.

- Explore physical activities that build strength and endurance and reflect upon how endurance exercise can challenge you to find a state of flow by allowing you to feel engaged. The experiences obtained from physical exercise can then be transferred to grow your mindset, allowing for increased endurance, agency, and self-worth.

Mars in Gemini

Mars in Gemini energizes communication, intellectual pursuits, and social interaction, infusing one's actions with curiosity, versatility, and adaptability. This placement encourages a dynamic approach to life, where ideas and information play a central role. The following suggestions could help explore how to work with agency and engagement for Mars in Gemini:

- Explore communication and increase your agency by expressing yourself and navigating social interactions. This can include speaking, writing, or learning new languages. Remember to challenge your mental ability as it can boost your sense of engagement to find a state of flow.
- Allow yourself to act on what makes you curious and reflect upon how that contributes to a sense of increased agency and fulfillment in your life.

Mars in Cancer

Mars in Cancer channels the assertive and dynamic energy of Mars through the nurturing, protective, and emotional lens of Cancer. This placement emphasizes security, emotional connections, and the home and family values. Below are some ideas for how to work with Mars in Cancer to increase one's sense of agency and engagement:

- Reflect upon what it means to act in accordance with your emotions and how that can foster a greater sense of agency and well-being by making you feel completely safe. Remember to act in accordance with your valued direction, avoid bottling up emotions, and instead try to approach your emotional self with courage and care.
- Explore what sparks your passion and dare to act upon whatever makes you feel engaged, possibly by trying out activities that have a nurturing aspect to them, as this can provide you with purpose while giving you a sense of belonging.

Mars in Leo

Mars in Leo infuses actions with play, creativity, and leadership. This placement channels Mars' energy into expressive and often public endeavors, frequently expressed through sport. Finding engagement and increased agency could potentially be done in the following ways:

- Take on leadership roles or initiatives that allow you to guide and inspire others, where your contributions can be recognized. Developing leadership skills can both enhance your sense of agency and make you feel more engaged through the challenges that might come with taking on a leading role.
- Dare to act upon your playfulness and incorporate that into your daily activities to spark engagement. Challenge yourself in a fun way to increase your overall engagement with life.

Mars in Virgo

Mars in Virgo channels the dynamic and assertive energy of Mars into meticulous, detail-oriented, and practical action. This placement emphasizes efficiency, precision, and utility, focusing energy on organization, health, and service. Below are some ideas for how to work with engagement and agency for Mars in Virgo:

- Try engaging in activities that require detailed analysis or meticulous craftsmanship, for example different kinds of crafts, writing, data analysis, or any work that benefits from careful attention to detail. Remember to add an element of challenge, and focus on precision to increase your sense of engagement.
- Act on your passion to help others in tangible and meaningful ways, as this could help create a sense of agency while providing a sense of purpose. Just remember to acknowledge what it is that makes you passionate about the act you carry out so that you do not forget yourself in the process.

Mars in Libra

Mars in Libra channels the assertive and active energy of Mars into areas governed by balance, harmony, and relationships. This placement emphasizes diplomatic engagement, fairness, and aesthetic pursuits, often seeking to resolve conflicts and create partnership-oriented solutions. Below are some ideas for how to increase agency and engagement through Mars in Libra:

- Act in accordance with your values by acting on your passion for causes that challenge you and promote fairness, justice, and balance. Actively working towards a cause that aligns with your values can increase your

agency and sense of satisfaction, providing a profound sense of purpose through passion.
- Explore your sense of agency by practicing acting on your own needs and balancing that with acting on the needs of others in both personal and professional relationships.

Mars in Scorpio

Mars in Scorpio channels Mars' assertive and dynamic energy into intense, focused, and transformative actions. This placement emphasizes depth, power, and resilience, often engaging in activities that contribute with depth and intensity. Some suggestions about how to explore increased agency and engagement for Mars in Scorpio include the following:

- Participate in challenging activities that involve some element of transformation or depth that involves investigating or turning around difficult situations. Doing so could allow for a greater sense of engagement but also reinforce your sense of agency by contributing to impactful changes.
- Increase your sense of agency by reflecting on how you want to express your power, both in your personal and professional life. Identify your values and try to act in accordance with them to make the most of your power by using your influence ethically and responsibly.

Mars in Sagittarius

Mars in Sagittarius acts with enthusiasm, a thirst for adventure, and a philosophical or expansive approach to life's challenges. This placement is characterized by a love for exploration and a desire to push boundaries and explore new horizons. Explore Mars in Sagittarius and the connection to engagement and agency through the suggestions below:

- Direct your energy towards projects or environments that challenge you while allowing for a high degree of autonomy, freedom, and self-direction. Sports are also favorable. Maintaining independence can increase a sense of agency, helping you to feel more engaged and satisfied.
- Reflect on how your values connect with your beliefs or moral compass, and dare to act in accordance with your truth to strengthen your sense of self and personal agency.

Mars in Capricorn

Mars in Capricorn channels the assertive and dynamic energy of Mars into disciplined, structured, and ambitious goals. This placement emphasizes practicality, endurance, and a strong drive for success. Mars in Capricorn could increase agency and engagement through the following suggestions:

- Practice viewing challenges as opportunities to grow and prove your capabilities. Tackling difficult situations with resilience and strategic thinking can enhance your sense of empowerment and achievement with an increased sense of agency.
- Establish clear, structured goals that are both challenging and achievable to feel engaged. Remember that the goals you set should be connected to your identified values, and passion should be your primary driving force for wanting to achieve your accomplishments.

Mars in Aquarius

Mars in Aquarius brings innovative, unconventional, and community-focused energy to actions and initiatives. This placement emphasizes individuality, intellectual engagement, and the pursuit of social reform or progressive ideas. Below are some examples of how to explore and increase agency and engagement based on Mars in Aquarius:

- Dare to act on your unique passions to increase your sense of agency. By acting on your passions, you can not only empower yourself but also contribute meaningfully to societal progress by acting on *your own* impulses, rather than conforming to societal norms.
- Explore ideas by questioning the status quo and act on opportunities that expand your knowledge and challenge your perspectives to spark progression. Expressing your energy intellectually can help keep you motivated and engaged, and increase your sense of agency.

Mars in Pisces

Mars in Pisces channels Mars' assertive and energetic nature into a more introspective, empathetic, and intuitive form. This placement often emphasizes emotional actions, a connection to spiritual or artistic pursuits, and a tendency to act based on feelings and compassion. Sparking engagement and increased agency could be done in the following ways:

- Explore acting in accordance with your values by incorporating your emotions or intuition as a compass to show you where to direct your energy. Your heightened sensitivity can help empower you to make decisions that are in tune with your very deepest values and to act in ways that are truly meaningful and help enhance your sense of agency.
- Express your passion for creative pursuits and allow yourself to feel fully engaged in activities that challenge you while contributing with a sense of formlessness, such as art, spirituality, dancing, or certain martial arts.

The Social Planets

Jupiter: Growth Mindset

After Mars, we reach Jupiter, and here we lift our energy (Mars) and turn it into a higher perspective. Jupiter is the planet that expands everything – a force that can create an abundance of all that we manifest. Jupiter's orbit is much larger than the previously mentioned planets, which is why it takes about 12 years for Jupiter to move in one circle around the Sun. Because of its larger orbit, we tend to refer to the planets from Jupiter and beyond as *generational* rather than *personal*. With Jupiter comes hope, expansion, faith, travel, learning, abundance, and happiness – but it requires us to use the drive we found via Mars to put our plans into action. Once we do, we usually get double the reward back as Jupiter expands everything we seek to grow. Keeping this in mind, we also need to remember that Jupiter can bring over-indulgence and tendencies to overstretch one's abilities. In order to balance these energies, we need to stay true to our core (Sun), express ourselves via communication (Mercury) so that our needs, values, and pleasures can be met (Venus), and then let the driving force (Mars) expand our plans to develop via Jupiter.

Before we begin to explore what psychological concept to pair with Jupiter, let us first explore how April Elliott Kent describes Jupiter as "your inner adventurer" and states how this planetary energy can be connected with several expressions of adventure, such as adventures of the mind (education), adventures of the spirit (religion), and physical adventures related to travel. Key concepts are presented as expansion, optimism, benevolence and the "higher mind," while Steven Forrest describes Jupiter as "the maintenance of faith," "the development of vitality and confidence," and "the lifting of spirits." He continues by asking some key questions related to Jupiter's influence in our lives, such as "What kinds of experience will help me feel more faith in myself and in life?" and "Where might I be taking too much for granted?"

When thinking about how to connect Jupiter to psychological concepts related to well-being, I found myself struggling because I think there are so many diverse concepts that would fit perfectly with Jupiter's energy. Some of them are hope, *active* hope, meaning, optimism, and growth. Interestingly enough, I am not surprised that I had so many options on my mind, as this is somewhat symbolic of Jupiter's expansive energy. Ultimately, I decided to go with the concept known as *growth mindset*, a construct developed by doctor and psychologist Carol Dweck that refers to the belief that one's abilities and intelligence can be developed through dedication, effort, and learning. Key aspects of the growth mindset include embracing the idea that personal qualities and abilities can be cultivated and improved over time by viewing challenges and setbacks as opportunities for growth and learning rather than as indications of limitations. A growth mindset involves believing in the capacity for personal growth and development over time and connects to Jupiter's optimism and faith, fostering a belief in the inherent abundance and potential for growth in oneself and the world.

Despite Jupiter's connection to optimism via the growth mindset, it is crucial to also mention that, as Steven Forrest points out, it is important to be mindful of times when we might be taking too much for granted. This statement mirrors that of growth mindset through the emphasis on effort, as the process of working with Jupiter is highlighted by balancing active dedication and perseverance with hope to foster a sense of purpose and tangible achievement. By embracing Jupiter and connecting it to the psychological concept of a growth mindset, we can begin to see life as an exciting journey filled with opportunities for growth, learning, and exploration. Based on what we now know, we can redefine Jupiter's key question to produce the following:

> "How can I expand and grow by incorporating a growth mindset in my life?"

Growth Mindset and Well-Being

In positive psychology, a growth mindset contributes to well-being by promoting resilience, a love of learning, and a proactive approach to challenges. Individuals with a growth mindset are more likely to embrace challenges, persist in the face of setbacks, and see effort as a path to mastery. This attitude leads to greater personal growth, achievement, and overall life satisfaction. A growth mindset encourages individuals to view failures as opportunities for learning and development, which can enhance their psychological well-being by reducing fear of failure and fostering a sense of control over one's life. This aligns with positive psychology's focus on enhancing human strengths and fostering a fulfilling life.[28]

Enhance Well-Being through Growth Mindset: Jupiter through the Signs

Below are some interpretations that could inspire you to begin reflecting on your own Jupiter placement while learning about how the astrological interpretation of Jupiter in each of the 12 signs can be practically expressed to foster well-being through the psychological concept of a growth mindset.

---

[28] Dweck, C. S. (2006). *Mindset: The new psychology of success*. New York: Ballantine Books.

Jupiter in Aries

Jupiter in Aries expresses a growth mindset through enthusiastic and proactive learning. Aries' natural boldness encourages taking on challenges head-on and viewing failures as opportunities for growth.

Jupiter in Taurus

In Taurus, Jupiter manifests a growth mindset by valuing steady progress and persistence. Taurus combines a love for learning with a methodical approach, emphasizing the importance of consistent effort.

Jupiter in Gemini

Jupiter in Gemini expresses a growth mindset through curiosity and adaptability. Gemini's intellectual flexibility allows for a love of learning and an eagerness to explore new ideas and perspectives.

Jupiter in Cancer

In Cancer, Jupiter manifests a growth mindset by nurturing personal and emotional development. Cancer's empathy and sensitivity foster a supportive environment for learning and growth.

Jupiter in Leo

Jupiter in Leo expresses a growth mindset through confidence and creative self-expression. Leo's enthusiasm for self-improvement is driven by a desire to shine and inspire others.

Jupiter in Virgo

In Virgo, Jupiter manifests a growth mindset through meticulousness and dedication to self-improvement. Virgo's attention to detail and analytical nature supports continuous learning and refinement.

Jupiter in Libra

Jupiter in Libra expresses a growth mindset through collaborative learning and balance. Libra values partnerships and harmony, seeing personal development as a shared journey.

Jupiter in Scorpio

In Scorpio, Jupiter manifests a growth mindset through deep introspection and transformation. Scorpio's intensity and determination drive a relentless pursuit of personal growth and overcoming obstacles.

Jupiter in Sagittarius

Jupiter in Sagittarius expresses a growth mindset through a love for exploration and broadening horizons. Sagittarius's optimism and adventurous spirit encourage a lifelong pursuit of knowledge and self-expansion.

Jupiter in Capricorn

In Capricorn, Jupiter manifests a growth mindset through disciplined ambition and strategic planning. Capricorn's practical approach emphasizes the importance of hard work and perseverance in achieving growth.

Jupiter in Aquarius

Jupiter in Aquarius expresses a growth mindset through innovation and progressive thinking. Aquarius's open-mindedness and visionary ideas promote learning and development in unconventional ways.

Jupiter in Pisces

In Pisces, Jupiter manifests a growth mindset through intuition and empathy. Pisces' compassionate and imaginative nature supports personal growth through understanding and adapting to the emotional and spiritual dimensions of life.

Saturn: Grit

After Jupiter comes Saturn, the planet with visible rings. The rings symbolize limitations and material structure, and the theme of limitation is also reflected through the notion that Saturn is the last planet we can observe with our naked eye. The power of expansion found through Jupiter needs to be materialized and concretized in order to be manifested — and this is where Saturn's qualities can come in handy. Saturn takes an average of 28–30 years to complete one orbit around the Sun, and Saturn rules all that is hard, material, and structural. What if you had no bones in your body? What would it be like if we did not have the concept of time to help us relate to existence? Also, consider how important it is to face resistance (Saturn) to expand (Jupiter).

Astrologer April Elliott Kent describes Saturn as "your inner teacher" and humorously connects its energy to that of Darth Vader. She mentions that Saturn rules limitations and tends to remind us that our actions have consequences and that "Life is hard. But you can't even begin to make it better unless you first face up to reality and take responsibility." Steven Forrest defines Saturn as "the development of self-discipline," "the development of self-respect," "the development of faith in one's destiny," and "making peace with solitude." He continues by asking some key questions related to Saturn's influence in our lives, such as "In what area of life must I learn to act alone?" "Where will a lack of self-discipline lead most quickly to sorrow?" and "Where will my ability to dream and have faith be most severely tested?"

When I think of connecting Saturn to a psychological concept that could foster well-being, I think of *grit*. Grit is a psychological construct defined as a combination of passion and perseverance for long-term goals, and it encompasses the sustained and focused application of effort towards achieving a goal despite challenges and setbacks. Grit involves maintaining interest and effort over extended periods rather than giving up in the face of difficulties. This concept was popularized by psychologist Dr Angela Duckworth, who identified grit as a critical factor in success, independent of talent or intelligence. Key components of grit include perseverance and effort through consistent and diligent work towards achieving a goal, even when progress is slow or obstacles arise. Grit is often talked about as a contributor to success in various domains, such as education, career, and personal achievements, as it emphasizes the importance of resilience, dedication, and sustained effort in achieving long-term objectives.

I think Saturn mirrors the psychological construct of grit through the representation of discipline, responsibility, and long-term commitment. Saturn and grit emphasize perseverance, consistent effort, and resilience in facing challenges. Saturn's energy is associated with hard work, structure, and the determination to achieve long-term goals, reflecting the same qualities of passion and perseverance central to grit. Just as Jupiter can help us grow, Saturn can also help us grow by having us confront and overcome obstacles on our path to personal growth and development. This is why grit could be thought of as a form of maturity, which further connects back to Forrest's definition of Saturn as "the development of faith in one's destiny." Faith in one's destiny might be increased or restored as we mature and learn that we can grow through resistance. In psychology, a person applying grit to work through challenges can tap into their personal resources (Saturn rules resources in astrology) to regain hope and optimism (Jupiterian themes). This is also how we can connect back to Jupiter and the fact that Saturn can help us *make use* (Saturn) of our *hope* (Jupiter) and turn our optimism (Jupiter) into something tangible and real (Saturn). Now that we know a little bit more about Saturn and the connection to grit, let us begin to redefine the reflection question related to Saturn, based on one of Steven Forrest's suggestions:

> "How can I work with grit to meet life's challenges with greater optimism and gain maturity?"

Grit and Well-Being

Grit is linked to sustained success and fulfillment, which are key components of overall well-being. In positive psychology, grit contributes to well-being by promoting resilience, a sense of purpose, and the achievement of meaningful goals. Individuals with high levels of grit are more likely to persist through challenges and setbacks, leading to personal growth and a greater sense of accomplishment. Research in positive psychology supports the importance of grit in well-being, as studies have shown that individuals with higher levels of grit report higher life satisfaction and are more likely to achieve their long-term objectives, contributing to their overall well-being.[29]

Let us now reflect upon how we can foster greater resilience by understanding Saturn through the 12 zodiac signs.

Enhance Well-Being through Grit: Saturn through the Signs

Below are some suggestions of how grit, as defined by Angela Duckworth, could be expressed through the energy of Saturn in each of the 12 zodiac signs. Each sign's expression of Saturn's energy highlights unique pathways to demonstrating grit through perseverance and dedication towards long-term goals.

---

[29] Duckworth, A. L., Peterson, C., Matthews, M. D., & Kelly, D. R. (2007). Grit: Perseverance and passion for long-term goals. *Journal of Personality and Social Psychology*, 92(6), 1087–1101.

Saturn in Aries

Grit through Saturn in Aries could manifest as bold and determined action towards goals, with a relentless drive and courage to tackle challenges head-on.

Saturn in Taurus

Saturn in Taurus expresses grit through steady, patient, and persistent effort, with a strong focus on achieving tangible, long-term results.

Saturn in Gemini

Grit according to Saturn in Gemini could involve disciplined learning and communication, with a focus on acquiring and applying knowledge consistently over time.

Saturn in Cancer

Saturn in Cancer might apply grit through emotional resilience and nurturing dedication, with a strong commitment to family and personal goals.

Saturn in Leo

Grit for Saturn in Leo is characterized by disciplined creativity and leadership, with a focus on achieving recognition and success through sustained effort.

Saturn in Virgo

Saturn in Virgo tends to mirror grit in pursuits requiring meticulous attention to detail and relentless improvement, focusing on practical and efficient achievement.

Saturn in Libra

Saturn in Libra tends to express grit through disciplined partnerships and fairness, maintaining balance and harmony while striving for long-term relationship goals.

Saturn in Scorpio

Grit for Saturn in Scorpio involves intense focus and transformational effort, with a resilient drive to overcome deep-seated challenges and achieve profound goals.

Saturn in Sagittarius

Saturn in Sagittarius shows grit through disciplined exploration and philosophical growth, with a commitment to achieving broader understanding and wisdom.

Saturn in Capricorn

Grit for Saturn in Capricorn is the epitome of disciplined ambition, with a relentless and strategic pursuit of career and status-oriented goals.

Saturn in Aquarius

Saturn in Aquarius could channel grit through innovative and progressive efforts, with a dedication to achieving long-term social and intellectual advancements.

Saturn in Pisces

Saturn in Pisces tends to apply grit to activities that involve disciplined creativity and empathy, with a resilient commitment to spiritual or artistic goals and helping others.

Uranus: Authenticity

Uranus is the first planet discovered with the help of technology in the form of a telescope in 1781. Uranus's journey around the Sun takes about 84 years and from this we understand that this planet is, as previously described, more *generational*. Briefly described, Uranus symbolizes liberation, rebellious energy, the future, science, innovation, unpredictability, and individualism. Returning to the analogy of how the planets mirror the energy of our human existence, we can see how liberation is a natural consequence of having gone through Saturn's structural and materializing energy. Through resistance, frameworks, and structure (Saturn), we can become aware of how we want to break free and reconnect to more of our individuality (Uranus). It is also through Uranus that we find detachment from what no longer supports our need for freedom and individuality.

Astrologer April Elliott Kent describes Uranus as "your inner revolutionary" and connects this planetary energy to "awakening, invention, originality, science, the future, electricity, revolution, unexpected events, and natural disasters," and writes that "Whenever you see people rioting in the streets, marching for causes, or engaging in civil disobedience, you're watching Uranus in action." Steven Forrest defines Uranus as "the development of individuality," "the development of the capacity to question authority," and "the transcendence of cultural and social programming," and asks the key questions: "In what department of my life must I be most willing to function without social approval?" "Where must I learn to break the rules and follow my own path?" "Where will I consistently receive most misleading advice?" and "Which authorities am I destined to challenge and offend?"

When thinking about what psychological concept to connect to Uranus, the construct known as *authenticity* switched on in my brain like a lightbulb. Uranus rules electricity and sudden ideas, so I was not surprised that this connection came so effortlessly. The psychological concept of authenticity involves being true to oneself, expressing one's genuine thoughts, feelings, and values, and acting in ways congruent with one's true self. It encompasses self-awareness, honesty, and a commitment to personal integrity, allowing individuals to live in alignment with their values and beliefs rather than conforming to external pressures or expectations. Authenticity is characterized by how well we can understand and acknowledge our true thoughts, emotions, and desires (self-awareness), how well we can openly express our genuine feelings and opinions (honesty), as well as to what extent we can act in ways that are consistent with our true self and values (congruence). This concept has been explored in depth by psychologists such as Carl Rogers[30] who defined and emphasized the importance of congruence (authenticity) in achieving personal growth and psychological well-being, which focuses on strengths and virtues that enable individuals to thrive.

Uranus and authenticity connect through the themes of autonomy and individuality, through acting in alignment with one's own values and beliefs, independent of external influences, and in striving for liberation from societal constraints. This connects back to Steven Forrest's definition of Uranus as linked to "the development of individuality," "the development of the capacity to question authority," and "the transcendence of cultural and social programming."

The psychological concept of authenticity and the astrological energy of Uranus both emphasize the importance of individuality, innovation, and liberation from societal norms by encouraging us to embrace our unique qualities, pursue personal freedom, and challenge established conventions in favor of progress and self-expression. Interestingly, this is also how we can connect Uranus (authenticity) to the Sun via the self-actualization process.

Based on this, we can now go on and redefine Uranus's reflection question:

> "How can I express myself more authentically by following my own path?"

---

[30] Rogers, C. R. (1961). *On Becoming a Person: A therapist's guide to psychotherapy.* Boston: Houghton Mifflin Company.

Authenticity and Well-Being

Authenticity tends to promote well-being by fostering self-awareness, self-acceptance, and congruence between one's internal experiences and external behaviors and is often thought of as essential for achieving a meaningful life. Research in positive psychology further supports this connection, as authenticity is associated with positive outcomes such as increased life satisfaction, improved relationships, and better mental health.[31]

Enhance Well-Being through Authenticity: Uranus through the Signs

Each sign's expression of Uranus's energy highlights unique pathways to living more authentically, emphasizing different aspects of individuality and genuine self-expression. Below are some suggestions of how authenticity could be expressed through the energy of Uranus in each of the 12 zodiac signs.

Uranus in Aries

Uranus in Aries expresses authenticity through boldness and individuality. Aries' pioneering spirit and willingness to take risks reflect a true-to-self approach that breaks new ground.

Uranus in Taurus

In Taurus, Uranus manifests authenticity through a steadfast commitment to personal values and preferences. Taurus's authenticity is shown by remaining true to what feels stable and secure, even amid change.

---

[31] Harter, S. (2002). Authenticity. In C. R. Snyder & S. J. Lopez (eds), *Handbook of Positive Psychology* (pp. 382–94). New York: Oxford University Press.

Uranus in Gemini

Uranus in Gemini expresses authenticity through open-minded communication and intellectual exploration. Gemini's authenticity is characterized by a genuine curiosity and the free expression of diverse ideas.

Uranus in Cancer

In Cancer, Uranus manifests authenticity through emotional honesty and nurturing connections. Cancer's authenticity involves being true to one's feelings and fostering genuine relationships.

Uranus in Leo

Uranus in Leo expresses authenticity through creative self-expression and confidence. Leo's authenticity is demonstrated by shining brightly and embracing one's unique talents and individuality.

Uranus in Virgo

In Virgo, Uranus manifests authenticity through practical innovation and a commitment to improvement. Virgo's authenticity is shown by a genuine dedication to making things better and more efficient.

Uranus in Libra

Uranus in Libra expresses authenticity through fairness and harmonious relationships. Libra's authenticity involves being true to one's values of balance and justice while fostering genuine connections with others.

Uranus in Scorpio

In Scorpio, Uranus manifests authenticity through deep emotional truth and transformation. Scorpio's authenticity is characterized by a fearless exploration of one's inner depths and the courage to change.

Uranus in Sagittarius

Uranus in Sagittarius expresses authenticity through adventurous exploration and philosophical honesty. Sagittarius's authenticity is shown by a commitment to discovering and living by one's own truths.

Uranus in Capricorn

In Capricorn, Uranus manifests authenticity through disciplined innovation and integrity. Capricorn's authenticity involves staying true to one's ambitions and ethical standards while embracing new approaches.

Uranus in Aquarius

Uranus in Aquarius expresses authenticity through individuality and visionary ideals. Aquarius's authenticity is characterized by a commitment to being true to oneself and championing progressive causes.

Uranus in Pisces

In Pisces, Uranus manifests authenticity through intuitive creativity and compassionate understanding. Pisces' authenticity involves embracing one's imaginative and empathetic nature in a genuine and heartfelt manner.

Neptune: Self-Transcendence

Neptune is a large planet made up of gas. Upon discovery, it is said that Neptune appeared and showed itself a few times, only to then disappear mysteriously from our human observation. Because of this, scientists first hesitated to determine whether a new planet had indeed been found.

This symbolism is reflected in the astrological understanding of Neptune as symbolic of mystery. Neptune symbolizes mystery, dreams, art, dance, music, romance, beauty, and spirituality. Neptune rules all that is formless, such as alcohol, gas, and oil. The formless description also fits well if we try to understand Neptune's reflection within ourselves. When we break free (Uranus) from rules and limitations (Saturn), a world beyond the physical (Neptune) awaits. Neptune, therefore, symbolizes our need for spirituality and formlessness.

My understanding of Neptune has changed a lot over the years. I am born with Neptune in the first house, which makes Neptune's energy prominent for my self-expression and personal identity. Just as with all planetary energies, we can identify a wide range of expressions related to the archetypes, and I strongly believe that the energies in a chart need to be understood from a more holistic point of view, which requires me to work both with Saturnian themes of boundaries and grit, Sun-related themes such as identity and self-actualization, while also adhering to Neptunian concepts of boundlessness, empathy, and formlessness. To sum it up, I believe Neptune can teach us how to connect to the world and formless themes such as fantasy, romance, empathy, imagination, intuition, and spirituality.

April Elliott Kent describes Neptune as "your inner angel" and states that the energy of Neptune is associated with spirituality, compassion, unconditional love, empathy, art, and psychic sensitivity. Steven Forrest defines Neptune as "the decentralization of ego in self-imagery," "the creation of a point of self-observation external to ego," "the weakening of the barrier separating conscious from unconscious, ego from soul," and "the development of an awareness of what we may call God." Neptune's key questions are stated as "Where must I learn to deemphasize logic and to function intuitively?" "Where is narrow self-interest most inappropriate and destructive to me?" "Where am I most vulnerable to mistaking wishes and fears for reality?"

In psychological terms, our understanding of Neptune could be linked to the concept known as *self-transcendence,* which symbolizes transcending the ego, or the sense of individual self, to merge with a greater whole in order to experience a profound connection with the world, nature, or the divine. Self-transcendence comes from the well-known *hierarchy of needs,* which was established by American psychologist Abraham Maslow in 1962.

First, self-actualization was stated as the highest human need, which connects to our understanding of the Sun. Later, the hierarchy of needs was updated to include *self-transcendence* as the highest achieved human need. This might

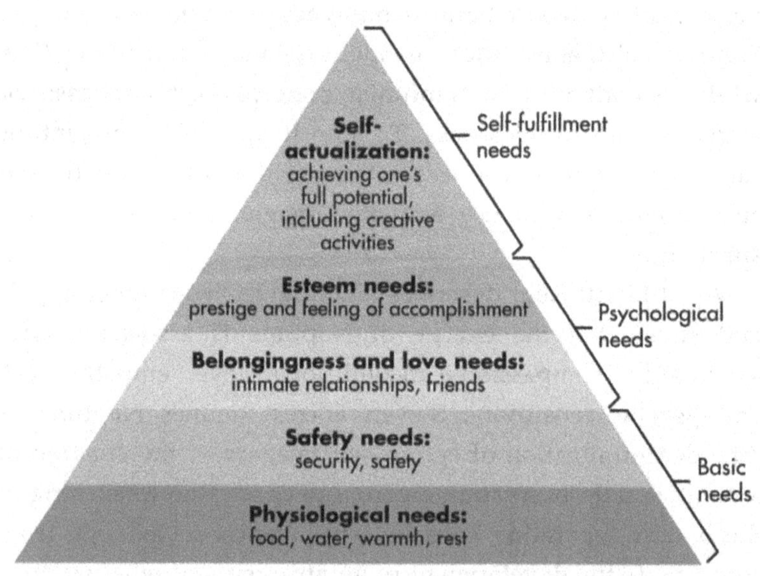

Maslow's hierarchy of needs, developed in 1962

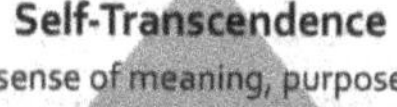

Maslow's updated hierarchy of needs, presented in 1969

sound like a paradox, but recent findings actually suggest that self-actualizing individuals are able to merge better with a common humanity through self-transcendence while also maintaining a strong identity and sense of self.[16]

Self-transcendence can help us explore altruism and compassion by exhibiting a greater sense of empathy, compassion, and altruism towards others. In general terms, this construct points to the ability to rise above or beyond the self and instead relate to something greater through the realization that we are a small part of a greater whole. This links with Steven Forrest's description of "the decentralization of ego in self-imagery," "the creation of a point of self-observation external to ego," and "the weakening of the barrier separating conscious from unconscious, ego from soul," symbolizing how Neptune can help us transcend ourselves and experiences ourselves as part of humanity rather than as *a human*. Interestingly enough, this makes me think of how Neptune also rules the ocean, which is made of small drops forming a massive sea together. In Neptunian terms, our understanding of humanity could be viewed similarly – we are all individual drops in a large ocean called humanity. Both self-transcendence and Neptune emphasize moving beyond the individual self to experience a greater unity and connection by highlighting the potential for profound spiritual experiences, compassion, and a heightened awareness. Based on this, we are now at the point where we will redefine Neptune's reflection question, which produces the following:

> "How can I transcend myself and increase my spirituality by connecting to unity, oneness, and compassion?"

Self-Transcendence and Well-Being

Self-transcendence is linked to well-being through its emphasis on finding meaning, purpose, and connection beyond personal interests. Self-transcendence encourages individuals to engage in activities that benefit others and contribute to the greater good, which has been shown to enhance personal well-being and life satisfaction. Research studies have shown that individuals who engage in self-transcendent activities report higher levels of happiness, life satisfaction, and psychological well-being.[32] The ability to go beyond the ego through self-transcendence also connects with the concept of wisdom.[33] In Abraham Maslow's theory of self-transcendence and needs,[17] self-actualization, that is, the realization of one's full potential, used to be considered the most prominent human need as it was placed at the top of the pyramid consisting of physiological needs at the very

---

[32] Kashdan, T. B., & McKnight, P. E. (2013). Commitment to a purpose in life: An antidote to the suffering by individuals with social anxiety disorder. *Emotion, 13*(6), 1150.

[33] Curnow, T. (1999). *Wisdom, Intuition, and Ethics*. Aldershot, UK: Ashgate.

bottom, followed by safety, love/belonging, and esteem. In the updated version, self-transcendence has come to symbolize the next level of human development as it is focused on pursuits that extend from the self and concern some kind of higher goal and purpose than those that are self-serving. Maslow describes it like this:

> Self-transcendence refers to the very highest and most inclusive or holistic levels of human consciousness, behaving and relating, as ends rather than means, to oneself, to significant others, to human beings in general, to other species, to nature, and to the cosmos.

Enhance Well-Being through Self-Transcendence: Neptune through the Signs

Let us continue by exploring how self-transcendence could be expressed through the energy of Neptune in each of the 12 zodiac signs.

Neptune in Aries

Neptune in Aries could express self-transcendence through pioneering spiritual quests and selfless acts of courage, using boldness to inspire and uplift others.

Neptune in Taurus

In Taurus, Neptune manifests self-transcendence by finding deep spiritual meaning in nature, beauty, and the physical world, fostering a sense of peace and contentment.

Neptune in Gemini

Neptune in Gemini expresses self-transcendence through communication and intellectual exploration, using creativity and imagination to connect with others on a higher level.

Neptune in Cancer

Self-transcendence in Cancer involves deep empathy and nurturing, with a focus on creating emotional bonds and supporting others through compassionate care.

Neptune in Leo

Neptune in Leo expresses self-transcendence through artistic expression and creativity, using personal talents to inspire and bring others joy, fostering unity.

Neptune in Virgo

In Virgo, Neptune manifests self-transcendence by dedicating oneself to service and healing, finding spiritual fulfillment in helping others and improving the world.

Neptune in Libra

Neptune in Libra expresses self-transcendence through fostering harmony and balance in relationships, using diplomacy and compassion to create meaningful connections.

Neptune in Scorpio

Self-transcendence in Scorpio involves deep emotional and spiritual transformation, with a focus on healing and rebirth, often through exploring the mysteries of life.

Neptune in Sagittarius

Neptune in Sagittarius expresses self-transcendence through seeking higher knowledge and spiritual truths, using exploration and adventure to connect with the divine.

Neptune in Capricorn

In Capricorn, Neptune manifests self-transcendence by integrating spiritual values into practical goals, finding purpose in contributing to the greater good through disciplined effort.

Neptune in Aquarius

Neptune in Aquarius expresses self-transcendence through visionary ideals and humanitarian efforts, using innovation and community focus to create a better world.

Neptune in Pisces

Self-transcendence in Pisces involves profound empathy, intuition, and spiritual connection, with a focus on merging with the collective consciousness and fostering universal compassion.

Pluto: Resilience and Post-Traumatic Growth

At last, we have come to Pluto — the celestial body that science no longer considers a planet but which, despite this, still has significant influence and meaning in astrology. The name Pluto connects to Greek mythology and means "Lord of the underworld." Pluto's irregular orbit of approximately 248 years makes Pluto a *generational planet* as it spends between 12 and 31 years in each zodiac sign. This enables us to see generations and large groups of people connected to Pluto in a certain sign, impacting large groups of humans on a mass-scale level. Pluto's energy is often understood through the myth of the phoenix rising from the ashes, which has its roots in ancient Greece where the phoenix was a mythical bird known for its ability to be reborn from its own ashes through immortality and the capacity to renew itself, no matter what. The developmental process that comes via Pluto requires us to explore our formlessness through self-transcendence (Neptune) so that we can shed light on our most inherent power (Pluto) through transformation, by having explored the deepest corners of ourselves. Once we have dug up all that is due to be transformed, we can then begin our journey back towards our center again (the Sun).

Astrologer April Elliott Kent writes that we can use Pluto's transformative cycles to gain insight, strength, and confidence and that its long orbit around the Sun symbolizes the kind of deep, transformative changes that really take time to unfold. Furthermore, Pluto's function can be understood as "our ability to face hard truths" as well as "our willingness to be transformed by some of life's most difficult experiences." Pluto tends to influence us with an energy that can make us taste the limits of our abilities in regard to what influence we have in our own lives, often to the point where life might be experienced as painful, unpleasant, and unfair — but this also can lead to immense transformative power in terms of deep, mature enlightenment. Steven Forrest defines Pluto as "the realization of one's destiny," "the recognition of the absurdity of all narrow pursuits," and "the development of the capacity to discern truth." He continues by asking some key questions related to Pluto's influence in our lives: "Where can I find enduring significance in my life?" "Where in myself might I find wisdom for which there is a great need in the world around me?" and "Where must I guard against dogmatic, unscrupulous, or tyrannical behavior?"

I believe *post-traumatic growth* makes a good fit when aiming to mirror Pluto's energy with psychology. This is because both Pluto and post-traumatic growth focus on the potential for personal growth, empowerment, and spiritual development in the face of trauma or crisis. The psychological construct of post-traumatic growth involves positive psychological changes that emerge as a result of having struggled with highly challenging life circumstances. Post-traumatic growth includes turning trauma into growth, which mirrors Pluto's symbolic death-rebirth process, where the old self transforms into a new, stronger self. Post-traumatic growth often requires confronting and integrating difficult emotions and experiences. April Elliott Kent's description of Pluto as representative of "our willingness to be transformed by some of life's most difficult experiences" connects post-traumatic growth to Pluto. In conclusion, Pluto's astrological energy of transformation, deep introspection, and rebirth closely mirrors the psychological construct of post-traumatic growth, reflecting the profound changes and new strengths that emerge from overcoming significant life challenges.

The other concept that comes to mind when thinking about Pluto is *resilience,* which could be argued to be a sub-component of post-traumatic growth. In modern psychology, the concept known as *resilience* is defined as "the process and outcome of successfully adapting to difficult or challenging life experiences, especially through mental, emotional, and behavioral flexibility and adjustment to external and internal demands."[34] This term is often characterized by a pattern of growth and positive coping after an individual has experienced major stress, for example, after losing a loved one.[35]

"Loss of a loved one" functions as an example of a situation that could lead to prolonged grief, but it needs to be mentioned that when we link research on resilience to the energy of Pluto, we do not necessarily talk about actual *physical death.* Instead, we can understand "loss" and "death" in a more symbolic fashion, mainly through the Plutonian keyword *transformation.* Here is also where the ancient mythology comes in handy as the phoenix rising from the ashes points to the process of renewal and being able to rise and come out stronger after facing situations that might have felt as if they were going to destroy us. As I bring forth this idea, I want to be clear that wherever Pluto is placed in your chart *does not* point to an area where you *will* experience physical loss or death. That is simply not how astrology works.

---

[34] American Psychological Association. (2024). Resilience. Retrieved 2024-04-23 from https://www.apa.org/topics/resilience

[35] Hatala, A. R. (2011). Resilience and healing amidst depressive experiences: An emerging four-factor model from emic/etic perspectives. *Journal of Spirituality in Mental Health, 13*(1), 27–51. https:// doi.org/10.1080/19349637.2011.547135.

Instead, I advocate for using the understanding of Pluto in our chart to make the connections to themes of trauma and traumatic experiences in a more subjective way. We might experience many deaths and rebirths over the course of our lives, despite being physically alive. This perspective connects to a more symbolic definition of the Plutonian process and calls for some kind of *philosophical* (Jupiter) or even *spiritual* (Neptune) understanding. Here is also where we can link our understanding of Pluto to astrologer April Elliott Kent's description of Pluto as a planet that can spark *enlightenment*. Steven Forrest also describes Pluto in terms of "the realization of one's destiny" with a key question involving the concept of *wisdom*. I strongly agree that there is something spiritual, enlightening, or destined about how Pluto manifests in our natal charts, although it might require time for us to see our Plutonian experiences from that perspective. In the book *The Power of Pluto*[36] the authors describe the Plutonian experience in the following paragraph:

> For each one of us, sooner or later, the Plutonian experience erupts from the depths of our souls. It comes upon us at different times, in the dark hours of the night, in the clear sunshine of day, in the fading twilight of the afternoon. Life batters and bruises us in many ways, and through it all, a basic pattern, a universality of experience, emerges. There are just so many things that can happen to us in this existence. We lose a beloved through death. We are rejected and abandoned by someone we love. We stand mute and helpless while a hard-won career shatters to pieces around us. We are stricken with a dread disease which extracts its terrible toll. Through it all, we have

[36] Robertson, A., & Wilson, M. (1980). *The Power of Pluto*. Farmington Hills, MI: Seek-It Publications.

> wrestled with grief and rage, the disillusionments, the agonies, the betrayals. We have all cried in the night. We have all made the journey into the depths of our being. We have – all of us – been there. And so, it comes upon us, this Plutonian experience. We realize the moment of decision is now. There is no one to help. There is no place to hide. The way out is to go within. Irrevocably, the starting point is up to each one of us, as we stand alone and unafraid, at the crossroads of Destiny. We make our choice, and having made it, a feeling of peace and serenity comes upon us. The fears of the future fade; faith in ourselves returns as we release the old self-defeating ways and joyfully open our hearts and minds to the new beginning. This is rebirth. This is renewal. This is the Plutonian Experience, and Pluto is the gut level of the soul.

Steven Forrest defined one of Pluto's key questions as "Where in myself might I find wisdom for which there is a great need in the world around me?" After having mirrored Pluto's energy with resilience and post-traumatic growth, we can now rephrase Pluto's question and ask ourselves:

> "Which of life's more intense experiences can I transform by observing them through a lens of gratitude and resilience in order to invite more growth and wisdom into my life?"

Resilience, Post-Traumatic Growth, and Well-Being

Positive psychology emphasizes human strengths and the capacity for resilience, aligning closely with the principles of post-traumatic growth. Studies have shown that individuals who experience post-traumatic growth report higher levels of life satisfaction, well-being, and psychological resilience.[37] If Pluto in the natal chart can help us identify and reflect upon our lives in terms of what has been challenging, intense, and/or even traumatic, how can we practically work with this energy in our everyday lives? And how can we apply a progressive and strengthening perspective rather than a somewhat destructive approach? One way could be through gratitude. It might sound strange to bring together the Plutonian concept of trauma or loss and link it to gratitude in this way. However, recent psychological research on this topic reveals that well-being can, in fact, be increased through practices involving gratitude[38] and that this can help mediate prolonged grief, for example when dealing with the loss of a loved one,[39] and that post-traumatic growth can emerge from grief.[40] To further consolidate this idea, we can apply the concept of gratitude and its mediating effect on prolonged grief and link it to Steven Forrest's questions "Where can I find enduring significance in my life?" "Where in myself might I find wisdom for which there is a great need in the world around me?" and "Where must I guard against dogmatic, unscrupulous, or tyrannical behavior?" From my perspective and experience, navigating through grief, loss, or trauma without applying some kind of hope or perspective of growth could indeed potentially make one become dogmatic,

---

[37] Tedeschi, R. G., & Calhoun, L. G. (2004). Posttraumatic growth: Conceptual foundations and empirical evidence. *Psychological Inquiry, 15*(1), 1–18.

[38] Elfers, J., Hlava, P., Sharpe, F., Arreguin, S., & McGregor, D. C. (2023). Resilience and loss: The correlation of grief and gratitude. *International Journal of Applied Positive Psychology, 9*(1), 1–19.

[39] Beckley, C. J. (2022). Gratitude and grief: An examination of gratitude in older men after the loss of a loved one [Dissertation, Antioch University Santa Barbara]. Proquest.

[40] Hurst, R., & Kannangara, C. (2022). Post-traumatic growth from grief — a narrative literature review. *Mental Health and Social Inclusion*. https://doi.org/10.1108/MHSI-09-2022-0059.

unscrupulous, or tyrannical — towards both oneself and others. This does not, however, mean that we should not be allowed to feel (see the section on the Moon and self-compassion as a reminder).

Enhance Well-Being through Post-Traumatic Growth: Pluto through the Signs

Pluto spends roughly 12–31 years in each sign, impacting generations of people. This is also why Pluto by house placement tends to give a more personalized interpretation, rather than just interpreting it by sign. Use the exercises at the end of this book to find out more about Pluto's energy in your chart. Below are some examples of how post-traumatic growth and resilience might be explored through Pluto in each of the 12 zodiac signs.

Pluto in Aries

Pluto in Aries could overcome trauma through bold and decisive action, and transform adversity into newfound courage and leadership abilities, by channeling their personal experiences into pursuits that inspire and lead others.

Pluto in Taurus

Pluto in Taurus could experience post-traumatic growth through developing greater resilience, patience, and a new, transformed deeper appreciation for life's simple pleasures. Themes related to one's self-worth could also be deeply transformed, by reflecting on one's resilience as a primary personal resource.

Pluto in Gemini

Pluto in Gemini transforms trauma into an opportunity for intellectual growth and communication to find healing through sharing their story, seeking knowledge, and fostering connections with others.

Pluto in Cancer

Pluto in Cancer channels Pluto's transformative power into deep emotional healing and nurturing. It grows by developing stronger empathy, creating supportive environments, and fostering closer family ties.

Pluto in Leo

Pluto in Leo could make use of post-traumatic growth through self-expression and creativity, transforming trauma into a source of personal empowerment and artistic expression, while shining a light on their journey and inspiring others.

Pluto in Virgo

Pluto in Virgo could grow through practical solutions and service to others. It could transform traumatic experiences to spark self-improvement and health while helping others heal and gain a deeper sense of purpose.

Pluto in Libra

Pluto in Libra's post-traumatic growth could emerge from exploring how to regain balance and harmony after traumatic experiences. Adversity could be transformed into a greater understanding of the profound power of relationships and fairness by advocating for justice and peace.

Pluto in Scorpio

Pluto in Scorpio experiences profound transformation through intense introspection and emotional depth by turning traumatic or intense experiences into a powerful catalyst for rebirth, healing, and personal empowerment.

Pluto in Sagittarius

Pluto in Sagittarius favors philosophical exploration and a quest for meaning to grow past traumatic experiences. By transforming trauma into "experience," they can expand their worldview, gain greater wisdom, and have a deeper sense of what it means to be human.

Pluto in Capricorn

Pluto in Capricorn channels Pluto's transformative energy into immense resilience and growth by realizing that "what doesn't kill you makes you stronger... eventually." Through discipline, ambition, and time, they can overcome any obstacles and build lasting foundations, no matter what.

Pluto in Aquarius

Pluto in Aquarius could experience post-traumatic growth through innovation and social change by transforming traumatic experiences into a force for societal progress and humanitarianism, thereby developing unique solutions and new innovative ways to transform experiences.

Pluto in Pisces

Pluto in Pisces could find post-traumatic growth through spiritual awakenings and by regaining compassion after adverse or traumatic experiences. Traumatic or intense experiences could be transformed into a deeper connection with the divine, enhanced creativity, and a greater ability to empathize and heal others.

Chapter 4

Practical Exercises and Chart Examples

How to Begin Working with Your Astrological Life Compass

If you are new to astrology, then you must probably begin by calculating your chart. This requires you to know the date, exact time, and location of your birth. Once you have that data, you can download an astrology app and insert your data or visit any of the existing websites to calculate your chart.

Whenever I teach astrology to beginners, I highlight the importance of patience and not rushing with interpretations. It's so easy to get lost in all the energies and how they might be expressed, particularly since we might be eager to find out what we can learn about ourselves.

In this chapter we will start by looking at the horoscope as your unique life compass by identifying the 12 life areas (i.e. houses) and approach the horoscope with curiosity. What does your horoscope look like? Are most planets on one side of the horoscope, or are they spread out evenly? Can you identify the planets by their glyphs and define which house they are located in?

Glyph Keys

The illustrations below show a glyph key for the 12 zodiac signs and for the planets. The basis of learning the astrological language lies in being able to read the glyphs. What is the first step if we want to read a novel? Learning how to read! The same goes for astrology. In order to read a horoscope, we must first learn the astrological language, which consists of glyphs and symbols. The part below will prepare you for the next sections,

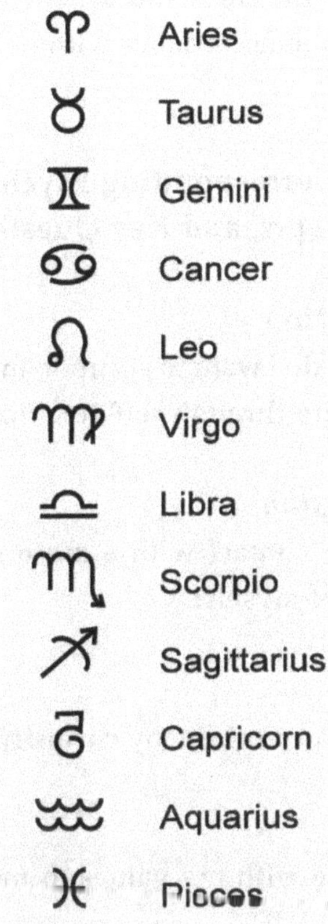

Glyph key: the zodiac signs

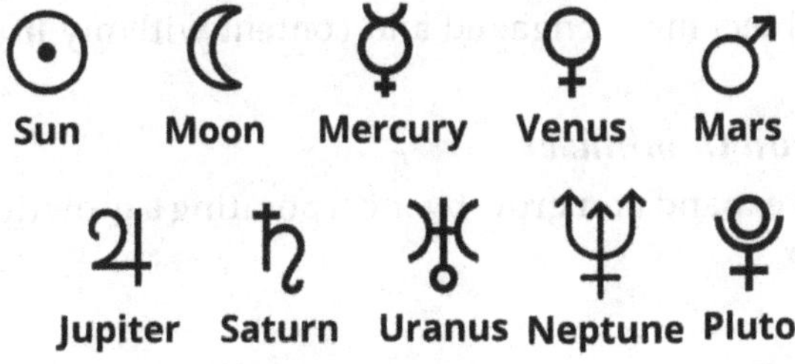

Glyph key: the planets

in which we will focus more on *how* to work with the identified planetary energies in the chart and use them to spark reflection and commit to action in accordance with our values and valued life direction.

Planets, Corresponding Psychological Concepts, and Key Questions

Sun: self-actualization
"What kind of values do I want to act upon in order to strengthen and clarify my identity through self-actualization?"

Moon: self-compassion
"How can I come in contact with a more nurturing and self-compassionate side of myself?"

Mercury: curiosity
"How do I express and explore my curiosity?"

Venus: harmony
"How do I act in line with my values to foster more harmony in my life?"

Mars: engagement
"What challenges do I want to commit to in order to increase my agency and feel more engaged and content with my life?"

Jupiter: growth mindset
"How can I expand and grow by incorporating a growth mindset in my life?"

Saturn: resilience
"How can I work with grit to meet life's challenges with greater optimism and gain maturity?"

Uranus: authenticity
"How can I express myself more authentically by following my own path?"

Neptune: self-transcendence
"How can I transcend myself and increase my spirituality by connecting to unity, oneness, and compassion?"

Pluto: post-traumatic growth
"Which of life's more intense experiences can I transform by observing them through a lens of gratitude and resilience in order to invite more growth and wisdom into my life?"

Identifying Energies and Life Areas

My Sun is in ____________ (sign) in the ____________ house.
My Moon is in ____________ (sign) in the ____________ house.
My Mercury is in ____________ (sign) in the ____________ house.
My Venus is in ____________ (sign) in the ____________ house.
My Mars is in ____________ (sign) in the ____________ house.
My Jupiter is in ____________ (sign) in the ____________ house.
My Saturn is in ____________ (sign) in the ____________ house.
My Uranus is in ____________ (sign) in the ____________ house.
My Neptune is in ____________ (sign) in the ____________ house.
My Pluto is in ____________ (sign) in the ____________ house.

A Chart Example

Now let's take a look at a chart example based on what we know about Mars' archetypal energy and the psychological terms "engagement" and "agency." We can aim for a more practical understanding by asking "What challenges do I want to commit to in order to increase my agency and feel more engaged and content with my life?" to the example chart below. There are, of course, many layers to this question, and there are many ways of approaching such a question when analyzing a horoscope. In

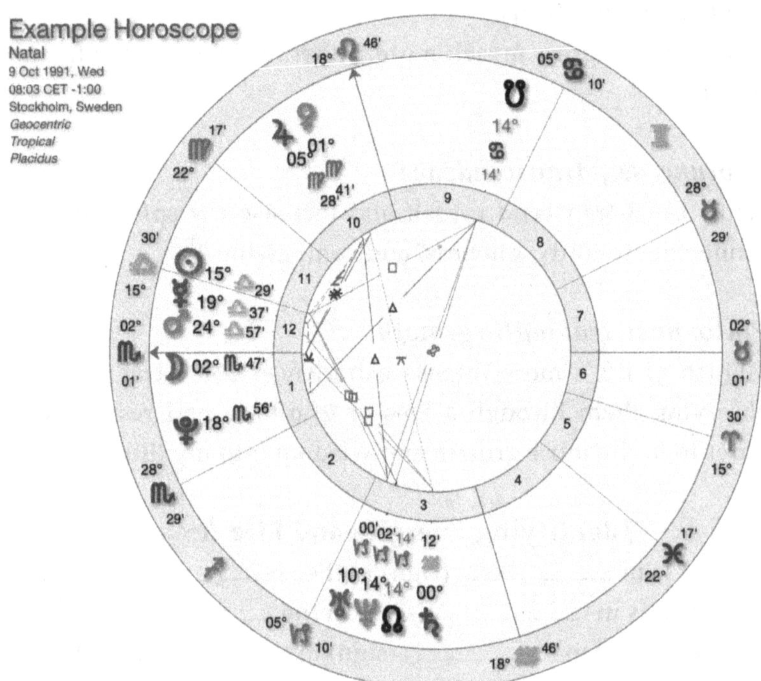

In the horoscope above, Mars is at 24°, 57′ of Libra, located in the twelfth house.

order to be pragmatic, we will start by zooming in on the planet Mars and analyzing it by sign, house position, and aspects. This will allow us to start reflecting upon Mars' question as we find a valued direction for how we want to direct our energy and passion.

Mars in Libra in the twelfth house

With Mars placed in the sign of Libra in the twelfth house we can first start to analyze Mars by sign. Mars in Libra is often passionate (Mars) about justice (Libra) and might be driven (Mars) in terms of diplomatic pursuits and harmony (Libra). If we were to look at our reflection question, we could already start thinking about how we relate to these concepts of justice and harmony in terms of challenges, action, and engagement. Could these kinds of themes be subjects that could evoke passion in a person with this placement? We could also look into other keywords linked to Mars and the sign of Libra as we strive to ignite reflection and create awareness. Astrology is a very creative practice, so we can allow ourselves to brainstorm at this initial stage.

When we add a house placement to this, we can see the kinds of areas where this kind of passion and drive (Mars) is being projected. In this case, Mars is in the twelfth house, emphasizing the life area of the twelfth house, also known as *the house of solitude, the house of spirituality,* or *the house of universal consciousness*. The twelfth house also rules our compassion for people who need help and understanding. It opposes the sixth house of our daily routines and habits, which makes the interpretation of this house more inclined towards dreams and experiences that are different from our daily tasks and everyday life. Based on this information, we can already make a simple interpretation and an attempt to answer the reflection question presented. This is also what is so intriguing about astrology — the fact that we can make a first initial interpretation, which we can later broaden and develop into infinity, all throughout our life. So, let's take a look at the reflection question again:

> "What challenges do I want to commit to in order to increase my agency and feel more engaged and content with my life?"

After having analyzed Mars by sign (Libra) and house placement (twelfth house), we can now say that one way that this native could feel more engaged and content with their life through their passion (Mars) for justice, diplomacy, and harmony (Libra) is in areas or life situations where the native

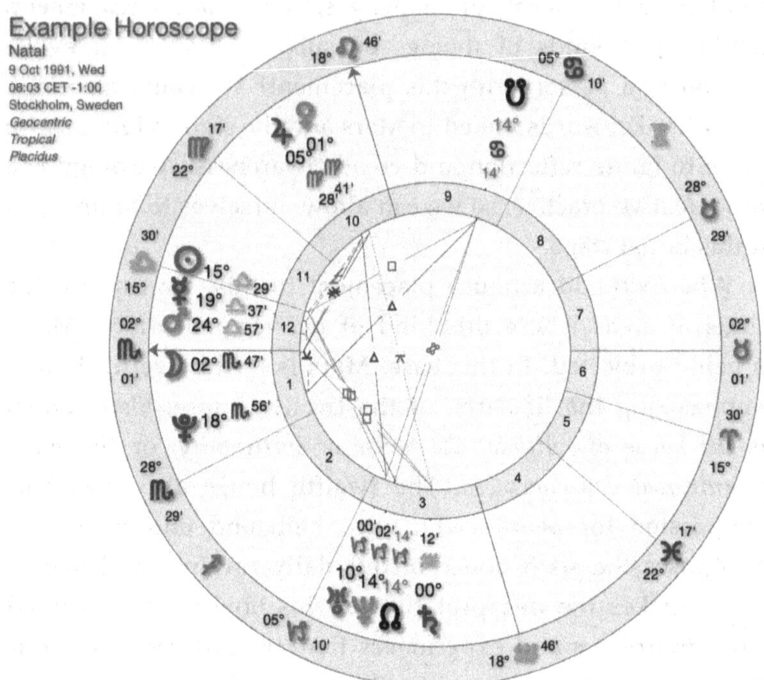

In the horoscope above, Mars is at 24°, 57′ of Libra, located in the twelfth house.

might come in contact with spirituality, mysticism, or people in need of compassion and understanding (twelfth house). For this particular individual, this was very true. Her main passions (Mars) revolved around helping those in need (twelfth house) in an attempt to create justice (Libra). However, this passion had been unbalanced for a few years, leaving the client with doubts about how to balance the passion for helping others, while also caring for herself.

Many think that astrological interpretations need to be complicated, which is not true. As the example above illustrates, we can start simple and build from there — just the fact that we now have identified that one potential way to express this person's passion, energy, and drive is through pursuits for the less fortunate (twelfth house), which includes some kind of act of justice (Mars in Libra). However, we do need to keep in mind that this is one potential interpretation and that there are, of course, many more interpretations of Mars in Libra in the twelfth house. But let's pause here in order to not over-complicate things too much at this stage.

House Rulers and How to Follow the Energies

We can now move on and also identify where the energies go and what houses (life areas) are connected to this person's passion and drive (Mars). In the example above, Mars rules the sixth house which begins at 18°, 13′ of Aries. The fact that Mars in the twelfth house rules this house creates a connection between the sixth house of daily work, routines, and health and the twelfth house of spirituality, self-transcendence, and mysticism. Analyzing this, we could say that the daily life or the work situation (sixth house) could be linked to or could include something related to twelfth-house areas. One potential interpretation of this could be that the daily work environment and the daily tasks (sixth house) need to be influenced by a passion for justice (Mars in Libra) for those less fortunate (twelfth house). The fact that this passion could be expressed through a job or vocation is also mirrored by the ruler of the twelfth house, which is the same as the ruler of Libra (Venus), located in the tenth house of career, vocation, and public role. This emphasizes the need to express the drive of Mars with something work-related that also includes twelfth-house themes.

Interestingly enough, the native of this horoscope had worked for a long time at different embassies where they had been focused on policy work, but they had lately started feeling a need to perhaps do something more rewarding such as working for a nongovernmental organization (NGO) or pursuing something that might help those in need in a way that felt more aligned. Knowing what we now know, let's revisit our reflection question again to see if we can add anything:

> "What challenges do I want to commit to in order to increase my agency and feel more engaged and content with my life?"

We can now add that the passion (Mars) for justice, diplomacy, and harmony (Libra) among people in need of compassion and understanding (twelfth house) is connected to the daily work situation (sixth house) and that the spiritual component of life (twelfth house) is related to a vocation or a public role (tenth house).

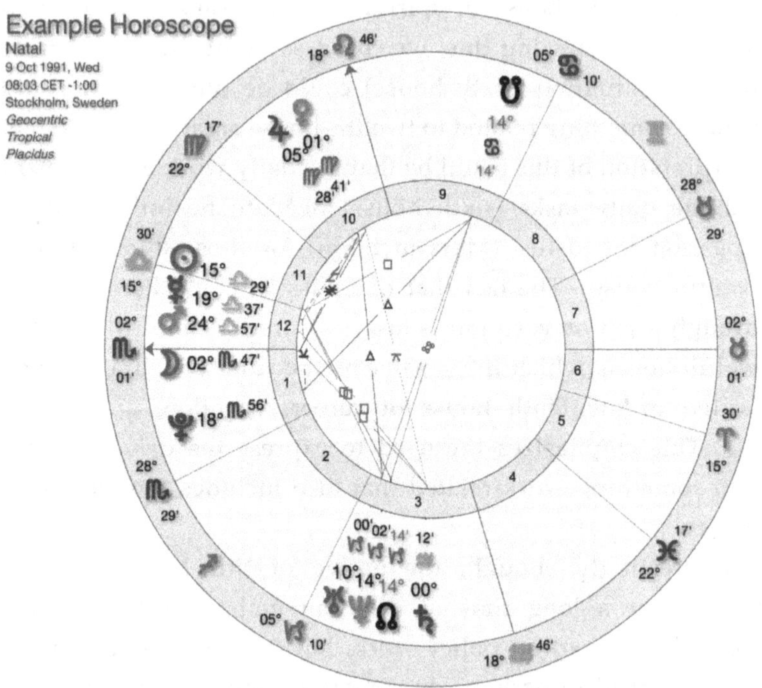

In the horoscope above, Mars is at 24°, 57′ of Libra, located in the twelfth house.

Defining a Valued Direction

The native with Mars at 25°, 37′ of Libra in the twelfth house might want to commit to challenges that allow them to feel more engaged through their passion and drive (Mars) for justice, diplomacy, and harmony (Libra) among areas or life situations where the native might come in contact with people in need of compassion and understanding (twelfth house). This could very well be done within a job role or vocation (Mars rules the sixth house, and the ruler of the twelfth house is in the tenth house).

This information can then help guide us towards redefining values and stating a valued direction, and that's how we also move on to taking committed action in accordance with our values, in particular since the energy of Mars has many sides and possible expressions. Reflecting upon Mars' influence in our chart could help us come in contact with our values and increase our awareness and agency by reminding ourselves how we want to channel that planetary energy to make the most out of it.

Practical Exercise I: Reflect upon a Planet

Now get your horoscope and begin to work methodically by following the steps below.

Step 1: Identify the energy

Choose an energy (planet) that you want to work with. Take a look at your horoscope and start by identifying where the chosen planet is by sign and house placement.

Example: I choose to work with Mercury in Taurus in the fourth house.

I choose to work with ______________________ in the ___________ house.

Then begin by making a logical interpretation and describing how the energy could be expressed.

Example: My curiosity (Mercury) wants to be expressed practically (Taurus) by exploring my roots (fourth house), themes related to "safety," physically in my home or in environments where I feel safe (fourth house).

____

____

Step 2: Intuitive/emotional reflection

Now we move on to integrating our logical understanding with our emotions and our intuition by complementing the logical interpretation with the help of our intuition and emotions.

Observe the sentence you just wrote and use your intuitive and emotional ability to interpret how the energy you identified is currently manifesting in your life right now. Are you letting it flow the way you wish? Write down what you receive through your intuitive reflection and emotional guidance.

____

____

____

____

Step 3: Set your astrological valued direction

Setting an astrological valued direction means that by identifying and reflecting on the energy in the horoscope, we can begin to express and manifest the energies in our life. Again, use your intuition combined with the logical interpretation to find what you value related to the chosen energy.

Ask yourself, based on your logical interpretation, intuitive/emotional reflection, current situation, and free will: How would you like to express the energy you identified in your horoscope? What values can be kept close to your heart and strived for, based on the themes you just identified?

Example: I value working and using my curiosity in the comfort and safety of my home. This means I value a job where I get space to work from home (Mercury in Taurus in the fourth house). I see myself sitting in my home (fourth house) writing (Mercury) books (long-term project = Taurus).

____

____

____

____

____

Practical Exercise II: Reflect upon a Life Area and See How Energies Connect

Step 1: Identify the house

Choose a house (life area) that you want to work with for this exercise.

Example: I choose to work with the eleventh house, by focusing on my values related to friends, community, and societal causes.

I choose to work with the __________ house, by focusing on my values related to ______________________________.

Continue by identifying what sign is on the cusp (beginning) of the house you choose.

Example: I choose to work with friends, community, and societal causes (eleventh house), which (in my individual horoscope) is ruled by Capricorn.

I choose to work with ______________________________
(__________ house), which (in my individual horoscope) is ruled by __________ (sign).

Step 2: Identify how life areas and energies connect

Now, proceed by identifying where the planetary ruler of the sign on the cusp of the chosen life area (house) is located in your horoscope.

Example: My eleventh-house cusp is in Capricorn, making Saturn the planetary ruler of my eleventh house related to friends, community, and societal causes.

My _______ house cusp is in _______________, making _________________ the planetary ruler of my _______ house related to ______________________________.

Locate the identified ruling planet by house.

Example: Saturn, the ruler of my eleventh house, related to friends, community and societal causes, is in the ninth house of development, education, and travel.

_________________, the ruler of my _________ house, related to __________________________, is in the ______ house of ________________________________.

Step 3: Logical and intuitive reflection

Then, begin by logically interpreting and describing how the energy could be expressed.

Example: In my horoscope, the life area related to friends, community, and societal causes is connected to the life area of development, education, and travel.

Proceed by integrating your logical understanding with your emotions and your intuition by complementing the logical interpretation with the help of intuition and emotions.

Observe the sentence you just wrote and use your intuitive and emotional abilities to interpret how the energy you identified is currently manifesting in your life right now. Are you letting it flow the way you wish?

Write down what you receive through your intuitive reflection and emotional guidance.

____

____

____

____

____

Step 4: Setting an astrological valued direction

Based on your logical interpretation, intuitive/emotional reflection, current situation, and free will: How would you like to express the energy you identified in your horoscope? What values can be kept close to your heart and strived for, based on the themes you just identified?

Example: I value connecting with friends and communities (eleventh house) that expand my worldview and inspire me to grow by exploring different cultures and life philosophies (ninth house).

____

____

____

____

____

Practical Exercise III: Reflect upon a Life Area Using a Planet

Step 1: Identify the energy

Continue by identifying any planets impacting the chosen life area. Remember that a planet symbolizes an energy that expresses itself through a *sign* and projects itself through you and into the outside world via the *house* it is located in.

Example: Uranus in Capricorn is located in my eleventh house related to friends, community, and societal causes.

________________ in _____________________ is located in my ________ house related to __________________________________.

Step 2: Logical and intuitive reflection

Then, begin by logically interpreting and describing how the energy could be expressed.

Continue by making an interpretation based on the identified planet and connect it to values related to the chosen life area.

Example: I can increase my authenticity (Uranus) by surrounding myself with unique individuals (eleventh house) who help me revolutionize my career path or public status to better align with my authentic ambitions (Uranus in Capricorn), perhaps through unconventional career choices or innovative business practices (Uranus in Capricorn) involving community causes (eleventh house).

I can increase my _____________________ (planet) by ______________________________________ (house) who help me __________________________________ (planet in sign), perhaps through unconventional career choices or innovative business practices (planet in sign) involving ________________________ (house).

Proceed by integrating your logical understanding with your emotions and your intuition by complementing the logical interpretation with the help of intuition and emotions.

Observe the sentence you just wrote and use your intuitive and emotional ability to interpret how the energy you identified is currently manifesting in your life right now. Are you letting it flow the way you wish?

Write down what you receive through your intuitive reflection and emotional guidance.

____

____

____

____

____

Step 3: Identify an astrological valued direction

Based on your logical interpretation, intuitive/emotional reflection, current situation, and free will: How would you like to express the energy you identified in your horoscope? What values can be kept close to your heart and strived for, based on the themes you just identified?

Example: I value connecting with friends and communities (eleventh house) that inspire me to grow by exploring my authentic ambitions (Uranus in Capricorn).

____

____

____

____

____

MANTRA
BOOKS

Recent Bestsellers from MANTRA BOOKS Are:

The Way Things Are

A Living Approach to Buddhism

Lama Ole Nydahl

An introduction to the teachings of the Buddha, and how to make use of these teachings in everyday life.

Paperback: 978-1-84694-042-2 ebook: 978-1-78099-845-9

Back to the Truth

5000 Years of Advaita

Dennis Waite

A demystifying guide to Advaita for both those new to, and those familiar with this ancient, non-dualist philosophy from India.

Paperback: 978-1-90504-761-1 ebook: 978-184694-624-0

Shinto: A celebration of Life

Aidan Rankin

Introducing a gentle but powerful spiritual pathway reconnecting humanity with Great Nature and arming all aspects of life.

Paperback: 978-1-84694-438-3 ebook: 978-1-84694-738-4

In the Light of Meditation

Mike George

A comprehensive introduction to the practice of meditation and the spiritual principles behind it. A 10 lesson meditation programme with CD and internet support.

Paperback: 978-1-90381-661-5

The 7 Levels of Wisdom

Mónica Esgueva

A straightforward and compelling approach on how to reach the highest levels of consciousness, wisdom, and inner peace.

Paperback: 978-1-80341-470-6 ebook: 978-1-80341-471-3

Compassion Based Living Course
Heather Regan-Addis and Choden
A practical guide to living a compassionate life.
Paperback: 978-1-80341-676-2 ebook: 978-1-80341-709-7

The Sacred Gathas of Zarathushtra & the Old Avestan Canon
Pablo Vazquez
The ancient and mystical poetry of Zarathushtra and the first Zoroastrians: Now accessible to the public in a modern translation.
Paperback: 978-1-78535-961-3 ebook: 978-1-78535-962-0

Radiant Bliss
Sue Bushell
Embrace Your Journey: Unfolding Peace, Power, and Purpose Through Yoga
Paperback: 978-1-80341-818-6 ebook: 978-1-80341-822-3

Ordinary Women, Extraordinary Wisdom
Rita Marie Robinson
The Feminine Face of Awakening
A collection of intimate conversations with female spiritual teachers who live like ordinary women, but are engaged with their true natures.
Paperback: 978-1-84694-068-2 ebook: 978-1-78099-908-1

The Riddle of Alchemy
Paul Kiritsis
What is alchemy, exactly? Is there any empirical truth to ancient speculative pursuits toward metallic transmutation? How does alchemy intersect with Western mind sciences and science in general?
Paperback: 978-1-80341-637-3 ebook: 978-1-80341-688-5

Readers of ebooks can buy or view any of these bestsellers by clicking on the live link in the title. Most titles are published in paperback and as an ebook. Paperbacks are available in traditional bookshops. Both print and ebook formats are available online.

Find more titles and sign up to our readers' newsletter at www.collectiveinkbooks.com/mind-body-spirit. Follow us on Facebook at facebook.com/OBooks and Twitter at twitter.com/obooks